Fundamentals of Information and Communication Technology (ICT)

FIRST EDITION

BY PRASUN BARUA

ABOUT

"Fundamentals of Information and Communication Technology (ICT)" is an informative and comprehensive exploration of the world of ICT. In this book, readers embark on a journey to understand the fundamental concepts, technologies, and applications that make up the vibrant landscape of ICT.

The book begins by introducing readers to the basics of ICT, tracing its evolution and highlighting its significance in the modern world. It explores the impact of ICT across various sectors, showcasing its transformative potential.

Readers then delve into the fundamental principles of computing, exploring computer hardware, software, data representation, and computer networks. The chapter on software and programming takes readers through the world of programming languages, concepts, and the software development life cycle.

Networking and Internet technologies take center stage in the following chapter, providing a comprehensive understanding of LANs, WANs, the Internet, and network security. The exploration of web technologies sheds light on website design, HTML, CSS, JavaScript, and the development of content management systems.

The book dedicates a chapter to database systems, covering the basics of databases, relational database management systems, SQL, and database design. Readers also gain insight into enterprise applications, including ERP, CRM, business intelligence, and e-commerce.

Emerging technologies are given due attention, with chapters devoted to artificial intelligence, machine learning, IoT, blockchain, and virtual reality. The book highlights their potential and explores their impact on various industries.

The societal impact of ICT is examined in detail, focusing on the digital divide, ethical considerations, privacy, cybersecurity, and online threats. Readers gain a broader perspective on how ICT influences society and the responsibilities it entails.

The book concludes with a look into the future, discussing smart cities, quantum computing, 5G, and the role of ICT in healthcare, education, and governance. It emphasizes the potential of ICT to shape a better future for humanity.

Throughout the book, readers are presented with practical examples, case studies, and real-world applications to enhance their understanding of ICT. The appendix provides additional resources such as a glossary of ICT terminology, recommended books, websites, and online courses to further explore the subject.

This book serves as an indispensable resource for anyone seeking to navigate the vast and ever-evolving world of ICT. Whether you are a beginner or an enthusiast, this book equips you with the knowledge and insights necessary to leverage ICT's power and make informed decisions in our increasingly digital world.

TABLE OF CONTENTS

CHAPTER 1: INTRODUCTION TO ICT

In this chapter, readers are introduced to the basics of ICT, its definition, evolution, and its vital role in the modern world. The chapter also explores the significant impact of ICT across various sectors.

Understanding the Basics: Defining ICT and Its Evolution

This section provides readers with a detailed exploration of the core concepts and the evolution of ICT.

The chapter begins by offering a clear definition of Information and Communication Technology (ICT). ICT encompasses a broad range of technologies, systems, and applications that are used for the creation, storage, retrieval, transmission, and manipulation of information. It involves the convergence of computing, telecommunications, and information systems to facilitate communication and efficient information handling.

Readers gain insights into the evolution of ICT, tracing its roots back to the early days of computing. The development of large mainframe computers in the mid-20th century paved the way for the initial applications of ICT. These mainframes, with their massive processing power, were primarily used by government agencies, research institutions, and large corporations for complex calculations and data processing.

The advent of microprocessors in the 1970s marked a significant milestone in the evolution of ICT. These microprocessors made it possible to create smaller, more affordable computing devices, leading to the emergence of personal computers (PCs). The accessibility and affordability of PCs democratized computing, empowering individuals and businesses to leverage ICT for various purposes.

Another key development in ICT's evolution was the birth of the internet. Initially, the internet was designed as a communication network for military and academic purposes. However, with the introduction of the World Wide Web in the 1990s, the internet became a powerful platform for information sharing and global connectivity. The web revolutionized the way people accessed and shared information, leading to the emergence of online services, e-commerce, and social networking.

Advancements in ICT also brought about the miniaturization of computing devices. The development of laptops, smartphones, and tablets enabled individuals to carry powerful computing devices in their pockets, further enhancing the accessibility and portability of ICT.

The evolution of ICT also saw the rise of cloud computing, which revolutionized data storage and processing. Cloud computing allowed users to access and store data remotely on servers, eliminating the need for local infrastructure. This shift to cloud-based services enabled scalability, flexibility, and cost-efficiency for businesses and individuals.

The chapter highlights the ongoing evolution of ICT and the emergence of new technologies, such as artificial intelligence, machine learning, internet of things (IoT), and blockchain. These technologies are pushing the boundaries of what ICT can achieve, opening up new possibilities and opportunities across various industries.

Understanding the basics and evolution of ICT is essential for readers to grasp the context and significance of the technologies and concepts that will be explored in the subsequent chapters. It lays the foundation for a deeper exploration of the fundamental components, applications, and societal impact of ICT, equipping readers with the knowledge needed to navigate the dynamic and ever-evolving world of information and communication technology.

Role and Importance of ICT in the Modern World

This section delves into the crucial significance of ICT and its pervasive influence in today's society.

The chapter highlights how ICT has become an integral part of everyday life, playing a pivotal role in shaping the modern world. It emphasizes that ICT is no longer confined to specialized fields but has become a ubiquitous presence, impacting various aspects of individuals' lives, businesses, governments, and society as a whole.

ICT has revolutionized communication, enabling people to connect and interact across vast distances in real-time. Through email, instant messaging, video conferencing, and social media platforms, individuals can easily communicate and collaborate with others globally, breaking down barriers of time and space. This enhanced communication has facilitated knowledge sharing, cultural exchange, and fostered a sense of global interconnectedness.

The role of ICT in facilitating information access and sharing cannot be overstated. The internet and digital technologies have democratized information, making it readily available to individuals across the globe. Through search engines, online databases, and digital libraries, people can access vast amounts of information on any subject, empowering them to learn, make informed decisions, and pursue their interests.

ICT has transformed the way people work and conduct business. It has revolutionized traditional work environments, enabling remote work, flexible schedules, and collaboration across geographies. With the aid of ICT tools and platforms, businesses can streamline operations, enhance productivity, and expand their reach to a global market. E-commerce has become a significant driver of economic growth, allowing businesses to reach customers worldwide and operate 24/7.

Education has been greatly influenced by ICT, bringing about significant changes in teaching and learning methodologies. Online learning platforms, digital educational resources, and virtual classrooms have made education more accessible and flexible. ICT has expanded educational opportunities, bridging gaps in geographical, economic, and social constraints. It has also opened up avenues for lifelong learning and skills development.

ICT has had a profound impact on healthcare, transforming the way medical services are delivered. Electronic health records enable seamless access to patient data, enhancing care coordination and reducing medical errors. Telemedicine and remote monitoring technologies enable remote diagnosis, treatment, and monitoring of patients, particularly in underserved areas. ICT has improved healthcare efficiency, patient outcomes, and has the potential to revolutionize personalized medicine and genomics.

Governments have embraced ICT to enhance service delivery and citizen engagement. E-governance initiatives have streamlined administrative processes, making government services more accessible, efficient, and transparent. ICT enables online service portals, digital voting systems, and citizen participation platforms, fostering transparency and accountability.

ICT has also had a significant impact on entertainment, media, and culture. Digital media streaming platforms, online gaming, and social networking have transformed the way people consume entertainment and engage with each other. ICT has allowed for the democratization of content creation, empowering individuals to express themselves, share their creativity, and contribute to the cultural landscape.

In summary, the role and importance of ICT in the modern world are multifaceted and far-reaching. It has revolutionized communication, transformed industries, facilitated access to information, improved healthcare, empowered individuals, and facilitated social and economic development. As technology continues to evolve, ICT's role will only grow more critical, driving innovation, and shaping the future of our increasingly interconnected world.

ICT's Impact on Various Sectors

This section explores the profound influence of ICT across diverse industries and sectors. The chapter highlights how ICT has revolutionized traditional practices, improved efficiency, and opened up new opportunities for innovation.

Education: ICT has transformed the education sector, offering a wide range of benefits. Online learning platforms, digital educational resources, and virtual classrooms have expanded access to education, enabling individuals to learn anytime and anywhere. ICT has facilitated personalized learning experiences, interactive content, and collaborative tools, enhancing student engagement and improving educational outcomes.

Healthcare: ICT has had a significant impact on healthcare, improving patient care, facilitating medical research, and transforming healthcare delivery. Electronic health records (EHRs) have digitized patient information, enabling seamless access and sharing among healthcare providers. Telemedicine allows remote consultations, providing access to medical expertise in underserved areas. Medical imaging technologies, data analytics, and artificial intelligence (AI) assist in diagnosis, treatment planning, and predicting health outcomes.

Business and Commerce: ICT has reshaped the business landscape, enabling organizations to streamline operations, improve efficiency, and expand their reach. E-commerce platforms have revolutionized retail, allowing businesses to reach global markets and operate 24/7. Supply chain management systems leverage ICT to optimize logistics, inventory, and distribution. Customer relationship management (CRM) systems enhance customer service and marketing strategies, fostering customer loyalty and business growth.

Communication and Media: ICT has transformed communication and media industries, offering new channels for information dissemination, content creation, and audience engagement. Social media platforms and online publishing have empowered individuals and businesses to share information, ideas, and creative content globally. Digital media streaming platforms have revolutionized the way people consume entertainment, providing on-demand access to movies, music, and TV shows.

Government and Governance: ICT has had a significant impact on government services and governance, improving transparency, efficiency, and citizen engagement. E-governance initiatives digitize administrative processes, enabling online service delivery and reducing bureaucracy. Digital citizen engagement platforms facilitate public participation in decision-making processes. ICT tools, such as data analytics and machine learning, assist governments in analyzing large datasets, informing evidence-based policies and enhancing public services.

Manufacturing and Industry: ICT has played a pivotal role in the manufacturing and industrial sectors, driving innovation, efficiency, and automation. Industrial Internet of Things (IIoT) technologies connect machines, sensors, and systems, enabling real-time data collection, analysis, and process optimization. ICT-driven automation and robotics enhance productivity and quality control in manufacturing processes. Virtual reality (VR) and augmented reality (AR) technologies assist in product design, training, and simulation.

Transportation and Logistics: ICT has revolutionized transportation and logistics, optimizing operations, improving safety, and enhancing customer experience. Intelligent transportation systems leverage ICT to monitor and manage traffic flow, reduce congestion, and enhance road safety. Fleet management systems enable real-time tracking of vehicles and optimize routes and fuel efficiency. E-commerce and logistics platforms streamline delivery processes, enabling real-time tracking and efficient supply chain management.

Agriculture: ICT has found applications in agriculture, driving the concept of smart farming. Sensor networks, satellite imaging, and drones assist in crop monitoring, soil analysis, and precision agriculture, optimizing resource usage and improving crop yields. ICT tools provide farmers with real-time weather information, market data, and expert advice, empowering them to make informed decisions and improve their farming practices.

These examples illustrate how ICT has permeated various sectors, revolutionizing practices, improving efficiency, and opening up new possibilities for innovation and growth. ICT's impact continues to expand as technology advances, playing a vital role in shaping the future of industries and society as a whole.

CHAPTER 2: FUNDAMENTALS OF COMPUTING

This chapter focuses on the fundamental concepts of computing. It covers the various aspects of computer hardware, software, data representation, storage, and computer networks.

Computer Hardware: Components and Architecture

This section provides a comprehensive exploration of the various components and architecture of computer hardware. Computer hardware refers to the physical components that make up a computer system and enable its functioning. Understanding these components is essential to comprehend how computers process data and execute tasks.

Central Processing Unit (CPU):

The CPU is often considered the brain of the computer. It performs the actual processing of data and instructions. This section delves into the architecture of the CPU, including its control unit, arithmetic logic unit (ALU), registers, and the fetch-decode-execute cycle. Readers learn about the CPU's role in executing instructions, performing calculations, and managing data flow within the computer system.

Memory (RAM):

Random Access Memory (RAM) plays a critical role in storing data and instructions temporarily while the computer is running. Readers gain an understanding of different types of memory, such as dynamic RAM (DRAM) and static RAM (SRAM). The section explores how RAM works, its capacity, access speed, and the relationship between RAM and the overall performance of a computer system.

Storage Devices:

This subsection covers various types of storage devices used in computers. It introduces readers to traditional magnetic storage devices like hard disk drives (HDD) and magnetic tapes, as well as newer solid-state storage devices like solid-state drives (SSD) and flash memory. The section explains the differences between these storage technologies in terms of capacity, speed, reliability, and cost. It also discusses the hierarchy of storage, including primary storage (RAM) and secondary storage (hard drives, SSDs).

Input and Output Devices:

Input devices allow users to enter data and commands into a computer system, while output devices display or present processed data to the user. This section explores a variety of input and output devices, including keyboards, mice, monitors, printers, scanners, and speakers. Readers gain an understanding of the role and functionalities of these devices in facilitating interaction between users and computers.

Other Components:

The subsection on other components provides an overview of additional hardware components that contribute to a computer system's functionality. It covers motherboards, expansion cards, power supplies, cooling systems, and peripheral devices. Readers learn how these components integrate to form a cohesive computer system.

Computer Architecture:

The section concludes with an exploration of computer architecture. It introduces the concept of the von Neumann architecture, which is the foundation for most modern computer systems. Readers gain insights into the structure and organization of the CPU, memory, and input/output subsystems within a computer system. They also learn about buses, which facilitate communication between different hardware components.

Understanding computer hardware components and architecture is crucial for comprehending how data is processed, stored, and communicated within a computer system. This knowledge enables readers to make informed decisions about hardware upgrades, troubleshooting issues, and optimizing computer performance. Moreover, it sets the stage for exploring software systems, data representation, storage mechanisms, and computer networks covered in subsequent chapters.

Computer Software: Operating Systems and Applications

This section explores the two primary categories of software: operating systems and applications. This section provides a comprehensive understanding of these software systems and their roles in enabling computer functionality and facilitating user interactions.

Operating Systems:

Operating systems (OS) serve as the backbone of a computer system, managing hardware resources and providing an interface for user interaction. This subsection dives into the functions and types of operating systems. Readers gain insights into the various types of operating systems, such as Windows, macOS, Linux, and mobile operating systems like Android and iOS. The section explores the core functionalities of an operating system, including process management, memory management, file systems, device management, and user interfaces. Readers also learn about the different types of user interfaces, such as command-line interfaces (CLI) and graphical user interfaces (GUI).

System Software:

System software is a category of software that works in conjunction with the operating system to provide essential tools and utilities for managing and optimizing computer systems. This subsection covers system software components like device drivers, firmware, and utility programs. Device drivers facilitate communication between the operating system and hardware devices, ensuring proper functioning. Firmware refers to the software embedded in hardware devices, such as BIOS in computers. Utility programs encompass a range of tools that assist in tasks like file management, data backup, system optimization, and security.

Application Software:

Application software refers to software programs designed to perform specific tasks or provide specific functionalities for users. This subsection explores various types of application software, including productivity tools, multimedia applications, communication software, web browsers, and specialized software for specific industries or domains. Readers gain an understanding of how application software enables users to create documents, manipulate images and videos, communicate with others, browse the internet, and perform various tasks based on their specific needs.

Software Development Life Cycle:

The section concludes with an overview of the software development life cycle (SDLC). It introduces readers to the process of developing software, including requirements gathering, design, coding, testing, deployment, and maintenance. Readers gain insights into the importance of proper software development practices, quality assurance, and ongoing updates and support for software applications.

Understanding computer software, particularly operating systems and applications, is essential for comprehending how computers function and how users interact with them. Operating systems manage hardware resources and provide a platform for running applications, while application software empowers users to perform specific tasks based on their needs. This knowledge enables readers to navigate software systems effectively, troubleshoot issues, choose appropriate applications, and make informed decisions regarding software usage and management. Additionally, it sets the foundation for exploring data representation, storage, computer networks, and more advanced topics covered in subsequent chapters.

Data Representation and Storage

This section explores the fundamental concepts of how data is represented and stored in computer systems. This section provides a comprehensive understanding of data representation, numbering systems, data storage technologies, file systems, and data compression techniques.

Data Representation:

Data in computer systems is represented using binary digits, known as bits. This subsection explains how bits are used to represent different types of data, such as numbers, characters, and multimedia. Readers learn about the binary numbering system, where each digit can be either 0 or 1, and how combinations of bits form bytes, which are the basic units of storage. The section also covers data representation techniques, including ASCII (American Standard Code for Information Interchange) for character encoding and Unicode for representing characters from different writing systems.

Numbering Systems:

In addition to binary representation, this subsection explores other numbering systems commonly used in computing. Readers gain an understanding of the decimal system, which uses base-10 and is familiar for human comprehension. The subsection also introduces the hexadecimal system, which uses base-16 and is commonly used for representing and manipulating data in computer systems. Readers learn how to convert between different numbering systems and understand the relationships between binary, decimal, and hexadecimal representations.

Data Storage Technologies:

This subsection delves into various data storage technologies used in computer systems. It covers traditional magnetic storage devices like hard disk drives (HDDs) and magnetic tapes, explaining their structure and working principles. Readers gain insights into newer solid-state storage devices like solid-state drives (SSDs) and flash memory, which provide faster access times and higher reliability. The subsection discusses the advantages, limitations, and trade-offs associated with different storage technologies, including factors like capacity, speed, durability, and cost.

File Systems:

File systems enable the organization and management of data on storage devices. This subsection introduces readers to file systems and their role in structuring and accessing data stored on hard drives, SSDs, and other storage media. It explores hierarchical file systems, such as the File Allocation Table (FAT) and New Technology File System (NTFS) used in Windows operating systems, as well as file systems like the Hierarchical File System (HFS) and Apple File System (APFS) used in macOS. Readers gain an understanding of how file systems manage file metadata, directory structures, and file permissions.

Data Compression:

Data compression techniques play a crucial role in reducing the storage space required for data and optimizing data transfer. This subsection explores data compression algorithms, such as Huffman coding, run-length encoding, and Lempel-Ziv-Welch (LZW) compression. Readers gain insights into lossless compression, where the original data can be perfectly reconstructed, and lossy compression, which sacrifices some data fidelity to achieve higher compression ratios. The subsection also highlights common applications of data compression, such as compressing files, multimedia, and network data transmission.

Understanding data representation and storage is essential for comprehending how computers handle and manipulate data efficiently. Knowledge of numbering systems, data storage technologies, file systems, and data compression techniques enables readers to make informed decisions regarding data management, optimize storage usage, and understand the impact of data representation on computing performance. This understanding lays the foundation for exploring computer networks, internet technologies, database systems, and other advanced topics covered in subsequent chapters.

Computer Networks and Internet

This section explains the infrastructure and technologies that enable communication and connectivity between computers. This section provides a comprehensive understanding of computer networks, network topologies, protocols, network devices, and the internet.

Computer Networks:

This subsection introduces readers to computer networks, which allow multiple computers to communicate and share resources. Readers gain insights into the advantages and purposes of networking, such as resource sharing, data transfer, and collaboration. The section covers different types of computer networks, including Local Area Networks (LANs), Wide Area Networks (WANs), and Metropolitan Area Networks (MANs). Readers learn about network topologies, such as bus, star, ring, and mesh, and their implications for network performance and scalability.

Network Protocols:

Network protocols are a set of rules and procedures that govern how data is transmitted, received, and interpreted within a computer network. This subsection explores common network protocols, including the Transmission Control Protocol/Internet Protocol (TCP/IP), which is the foundation of internet communication. Readers gain an understanding of how protocols enable reliable and efficient data transmission across networks. The section also introduces other protocols such as DNS (Domain Name System), HTTP (Hypertext Transfer Protocol), FTP (File Transfer Protocol), and SMTP (Simple Mail Transfer Protocol).

Network Devices:

This subsection delves into various network devices that facilitate network communication and connectivity. Readers learn about network interface cards (NICs), which enable computers to connect to networks. They gain insights into routers, which direct data packets between networks, and switches, which facilitate data transmission within a network. The section also covers hubs, repeaters, and modems, highlighting their roles in network communication.

Internet:

This subsection explores the internet, a global network of interconnected networks. Readers gain an understanding of the history and evolution of the internet, from its inception as a military and academic network to its widespread public use. The section explains the underlying technologies that enable internet connectivity, such as TCP/IP, IP addressing, and domain names. Readers learn about Internet Service Providers (ISPs) and how they provide internet access to individuals and organizations. The section also covers the World Wide Web (WWW) and introduces concepts like URLs (Uniform Resource Locators) and web browsers.

Internet Security:

This subsection highlights the importance of internet security and the challenges associated with maintaining secure communication and data transfer. Readers gain insights into common threats, such as malware, hacking, and phishing attacks. They learn about security measures like firewalls, encryption, and virtual private networks (VPNs) that protect network communication. The section also emphasizes the significance of user awareness, strong passwords, and regular software updates in maintaining internet security.

Understanding computer networks and the internet is crucial for comprehending how computers communicate and share information on a global scale. Knowledge of network protocols, devices, internet infrastructure, and security measures enables readers to make informed decisions regarding network configuration, internet usage, and data protection. This understanding forms the foundation for exploring web technologies, database systems, network security, and other advanced topics covered in subsequent chapters.

CHAPTER 3: SOFTWARE AND PROGRAMMING

This chapter provides an in-depth exploration of programming languages, programming concepts and principles, object-oriented programming (OOP), and the software development life cycle (SDLC).

Introduction to Programming Languages

This section provides readers with a comprehensive understanding of programming languages and their role in software development. Programming languages are designed to communicate instructions to a computer and enable the creation of software applications. This section introduces readers to the fundamental concepts of programming languages and explores their syntax, semantics, and purpose.

Purpose of Programming Languages:

The section begins by explaining the purpose of programming languages in software development. Readers learn that programming languages serve as a bridge between humans and computers, allowing programmers to express their ideas and intentions in a structured and understandable format. Programming languages enable programmers to write instructions that computers can execute, facilitating the creation of software applications to solve specific problems or perform specific tasks.

Types of Programming Languages:

This subsection provides an overview of the different types of programming languages available. Readers learn about high-level programming languages, which are designed to be more human-readable and abstracted from the computer's hardware. Examples of high-level languages include Python, Java, C++, and JavaScript. The section also introduces scripting languages, which are often used for automating tasks or developing web applications. Popular scripting languages include Python, Ruby, Perl, and PowerShell.

Syntax and Semantics:

The section explores the syntax and semantics of programming languages. Syntax refers to the rules and structure that define how code should be written in a particular programming language. Readers learn about concepts such as keywords, identifiers, variables, operators, and control structures that form the syntax of programming languages. Semantics, on the other hand, deals with the meaning and interpretation of code. It encompasses how statements and expressions are executed and how data is manipulated.

Choosing the Right Programming Language:

The subsection highlights the importance of choosing the right programming language for a specific task or application. Factors such as the requirements of the project, the target platform, the available libraries and frameworks, and the level of programmer expertise play a significant role in selecting the appropriate programming language. Readers learn that different programming languages have different strengths and weaknesses, and selecting the right language can greatly impact the efficiency and effectiveness of software development.

Evolving Nature of Programming Languages:

The section acknowledges that programming languages are constantly evolving to meet the demands of changing technologies and paradigms. It introduces readers to the concept of language evolution, including updates, new features, and community-driven advancements. Readers are encouraged to stay updated with the latest trends and developments in programming languages to adapt and leverage new capabilities for software development.

Understanding programming languages is fundamental to becoming a proficient software developer. This knowledge enables readers to write code, understand existing software applications, and collaborate with other programmers effectively. By understanding the purpose, types, syntax, and semantics of programming languages, readers are equipped to choose the right language for specific tasks and adapt to the evolving nature of programming languages.

The section on Introduction to Programming Languages sets the foundation for readers to explore programming concepts, object-oriented programming, software development methodologies, and advanced techniques covered in subsequent sections and chapters. It empowers readers to embark on the journey of software development, unlocking the power of information and communication technology to create innovative solutions and drive technological advancements.

Programming Concepts and Principles

This section discusses the fundamental concepts and principles that form the building blocks of programming. This section provides readers with a comprehensive understanding of variables, data types, operators, control structures, functions, arrays, and the importance of logic and efficiency in coding.

Variables:

Variables are essential elements in programming that allow programmers to store and manipulate data. This subsection introduces readers to variables and their role in programming. Readers learn about variable declaration, assignment, and naming conventions. They gain insights into different variable types, including integers, floating-point numbers, strings, booleans, and more. Readers also learn how to use variables to store and manipulate data during program execution.

Data Types:

Data types define the nature and characteristics of data in programming. This subsection explores various data types, such as integers, floating-point numbers, characters, strings, booleans, and more. Readers gain an understanding of the characteristics and limitations of different data types. They learn how to choose the appropriate data type based on the nature of the data being represented and the requirements of the program.

Operators:

Operators are symbols or keywords used to perform operations on data. This subsection covers different types of operators, including arithmetic operators, comparison operators, logical operators, assignment operators, and more. Readers gain an understanding of how to use operators to perform mathematical calculations, compare values, combine conditions, and modify data.

Control Structures:

Control structures dictate the flow of execution within a program. This subsection explores control structures such as conditionals (if-else statements, switch statements) and loops (for loops, while loops). Readers learn how to use control structures to make decisions, repeat actions, and control program flow based on specific conditions. They gain insights into the importance of logical expressions and conditional statements in controlling program behavior.

Functions:

Functions are blocks of reusable code that perform specific tasks. This subsection introduces readers to functions and their role in programming. Readers learn how to define functions, pass arguments, and return values. They gain an understanding of the importance of modular programming and code reuse, as functions allow for efficient and organized code development. Readers also explore the concept of function libraries and the benefits of leveraging pre-built functions to simplify programming tasks.

Arrays:

Arrays are data structures that allow programmers to store and manipulate collections of data. This subsection delves into arrays and their usage in programming. Readers learn how to declare, initialize, and access elements in arrays. They gain insights into the concept of indexing, array traversal, and the use of loops to manipulate array data. The subsection also explores multi-dimensional arrays and their applications in handling more complex data structures.

Logic and Efficiency:

This subsection emphasizes the importance of logic and efficiency in programming. Readers learn the significance of writing clear, concise, and logically structured code. They gain insights into best practices for code organization, documentation, and readability. The subsection highlights the significance of algorithmic thinking and problem-solving approaches in developing efficient and effective programs.

Understanding programming concepts and principles is vital for proficient software development. Knowledge of variables, data types, operators, control structures, functions, arrays, and the importance of logic and efficiency empowers readers to write code, solve problems, and develop robust software applications. This understanding lays the foundation for exploring advanced programming techniques, object-oriented programming, and the software development life cycle covered in subsequent sections and chapters.

Object-Oriented Programming

Object-Oriented Programming (OOP) is a programming paradigm that organizes software design around objects, which are instances of classes. The section on "Object-Oriented Programming" in Chapter 3 of "Unleashing the Power of Information and Communication Technology: A Comprehensive Guide" provides readers with a comprehensive understanding of OOP concepts, principles, and their practical applications in software development.

Introduction to Object-Oriented Programming:

This subsection introduces readers to the concept of Object-Oriented Programming (OOP). Readers learn that OOP is a programming paradigm that emphasizes the organization of code around objects, which are instances of classes. The subsection highlights the benefits of using OOP, including code reusability, modularity, and ease of maintenance. Readers also gain insights into the differences between OOP and procedural programming.

Classes and Objects:

This subsection delves into the core building blocks of OOP: classes and objects. Readers learn that a class is a blueprint or template that defines the properties (attributes) and behaviors (methods) of objects. They gain an understanding of how objects are instantiated from classes, and how each object can have its own unique set of attributes and behavior. Readers learn about the concept of encapsulation, which refers to the bundling of data and methods within a class, ensuring data integrity and abstraction.

Inheritance:

Inheritance is a key principle in OOP that enables the creation of hierarchical relationships between classes. This subsection explores the concept of inheritance, where a class (child class or subclass) can inherit attributes and behaviors from another class (parent class or superclass). Readers gain an understanding of how inheritance promotes code reuse, modularity, and extensibility. They learn about the different types of inheritance, such as single inheritance, multiple inheritance, and hierarchical inheritance.

Polymorphism:

Polymorphism is another fundamental principle of OOP that allows objects to exhibit different forms or behaviors. This subsection delves into polymorphism and its practical applications. Readers learn about method overriding, where a subclass provides its implementation of a method inherited from a superclass. They also explore method overloading, where multiple methods with the same name but different parameters can exist within a class. Readers gain insights into the benefits of polymorphism, such as code flexibility and extensibility.

Encapsulation:

Encapsulation is a concept that promotes data hiding and information hiding within objects. This subsection explores encapsulation and its role in OOP. Readers learn about access modifiers, such as public, private, and protected, which control the visibility and accessibility of attributes and methods. They gain an understanding of how encapsulation enhances code organization, security, and maintainability.

Abstraction:

Abstraction refers to the process of simplifying complex systems by breaking them down into more manageable and understandable components. This subsection delves into abstraction and its significance in OOP. Readers learn that abstraction allows programmers to focus on the essential features of an object while hiding unnecessary implementation details. They gain insights into abstract classes and interfaces, which provide a foundation for creating hierarchies of related classes.

Object-Oriented Programming is a powerful paradigm for software development. By organizing code around objects, classes, inheritance, polymorphism, encapsulation, and abstraction, programmers can create modular, reusable, and maintainable software applications. Understanding OOP concepts and principles equips readers with the skills to design and develop complex software systems, leverage existing code libraries, and collaborate effectively with other developers. This knowledge forms the foundation for exploring software development methodologies, design patterns, and advanced programming techniques covered in subsequent sections and chapters.

Software Development Life Cycle (SDLC)

Software Development Life Cycle (SDLC) is a systematic approach used to guide the development of software applications. This section provides readers with a comprehensive understanding of the different phases involved in the SDLC and the activities within each phase.

Introduction to SDLC:

This subsection introduces readers to the concept of the Software Development Life Cycle (SDLC). It explains that the SDLC is a structured approach to software development that ensures the efficient and effective creation of high-quality software applications. Readers learn that the SDLC consists of a series of well-defined phases, each with specific goals, activities, and deliverables.

Requirements Gathering:

The first phase of the SDLC is requirements gathering. In this phase, readers learn that the project team interacts with stakeholders to understand their needs and expectations. Activities in this phase include conducting interviews, gathering user requirements, analyzing existing systems, and defining the project scope. The deliverables of this phase are the requirements documentation, which outlines the functional and non-functional requirements of the software application.

Analysis and Design:

The analysis and design phase focuses on converting the gathered requirements into a detailed system design. This subsection explores the activities involved in this phase, such as creating system models, data flow diagrams, and class diagrams. Readers learn about the importance of creating a robust and scalable system architecture and designing user interfaces that align with user requirements. The deliverables of this phase include system design documents and prototypes.

Implementation:

The implementation phase is where the actual coding and development of the software application takes place. Readers gain insights into the activities involved, such as writing code, configuring databases, integrating components, and conducting unit testing. They learn about the importance of following coding standards, using version control systems, and collaborating effectively within the development team. The deliverables of this phase are the developed software modules and components.

Testing and Quality Assurance:

The testing and quality assurance phase focuses on ensuring that the developed software application meets the specified requirements and is free of defects. This subsection explores various types of testing, including unit testing, integration testing, system testing, and user acceptance testing. Readers learn about the importance of creating test cases, conducting regression testing, and tracking and fixing bugs. The deliverables of this phase include the test plans, test cases, and a high-quality software application.

Deployment and Maintenance:

The deployment and maintenance phase involves deploying the software application to the production environment and providing ongoing support and maintenance. Readers gain insights into activities such as installation, configuration, data migration, and user training. They learn about the importance of documentation, user support, and software updates. The deliverables of this phase include the deployed software application, user manuals, and support documentation.

The SDLC is an iterative process, meaning that each phase may be revisited and revised based on feedback and changing requirements. This subsection highlights the importance of project management, communication, and collaboration throughout the SDLC. It emphasizes the need for clear documentation, risk management, and stakeholder engagement to ensure the successful completion of software development projects.

Understanding the Software Development Life Cycle equips readers with a structured approach to software development. Knowledge of the different phases, activities, and deliverables enables readers to plan and execute software development projects effectively. This understanding forms the foundation for exploring software development methodologies, agile practices, software testing, and project management covered in subsequent sections and chapters.

CHAPTER 4: NETWORKING AND INTERNET TECHNOLOGIES

This chapter provides an in-depth exploration of networking fundamentals, internet protocols, network security and encryption, and cloud computing and virtualization.

Networking Fundamentals: LAN, WAN, and MAN

This section provides readers with a comprehensive understanding of the different types of computer networks: Local Area Networks (LANs), Wide Area Networks (WANs), and Metropolitan Area Networks (MANs).

Local Area Networks (LANs):

A Local Area Network (LAN) is a network that covers a relatively small geographical area, such as a home, office building, or campus. In this subsection, readers learn about the key characteristics of LANs, including their size, speed, and ownership. They gain insights into the components of a LAN, such as network switches, routers, and network interface cards (NICs). Readers also explore different LAN topologies, including bus, star, ring, and mesh, and the advantages and limitations of each topology. The subsection emphasizes the importance of LANs in facilitating local communication, resource sharing, and data transfer within a confined area.

Wide Area Networks (WANs):

A Wide Area Network (WAN) is a network that spans a large geographical area, connecting multiple LANs or other networks together. This subsection introduces readers to WANs and their role in enabling long-distance communication. Readers gain an understanding of WAN technologies, such as leased lines, circuit-switched networks, and packet-switched networks. They learn about the importance of WAN protocols, such as the Internet Protocol (IP) and the role of routers in facilitating data transmission across WANs. The subsection highlights the significance of WANs in connecting geographically dispersed locations, enabling global communication, and supporting internet connectivity.

Metropolitan Area Networks (MANs):

A Metropolitan Area Network (MAN) is a network that spans a city or metropolitan area, providing connectivity between LANs and WANs. In this subsection, readers explore the characteristics and applications of MANs. They gain insights into the technologies used in MANs, such as fiber optics, wireless communication, and high-speed Ethernet. The subsection emphasizes the importance of MANs in facilitating communication between different organizations, government entities, and educational institutions within a city or region.

Network Infrastructure:

This subsection delves into the components and infrastructure required to establish and maintain computer networks. Readers learn about network devices such as switches, routers, network cables, and wireless access points. They gain an understanding of network protocols, including Ethernet and Wi-Fi, which enable data transmission over the network infrastructure. The subsection also covers network addressing, including IP addressing and subnetting, and the role of network administrators in managing and maintaining network infrastructure.

Understanding networking fundamentals, including LANs, WANs, and MANs, is crucial for designing, implementing, and managing computer networks. Knowledge of different network types, their characteristics, and components enables readers to make informed decisions regarding network architecture, scalability, and performance. It also provides a foundation for exploring advanced networking concepts such as network security, routing protocols, and network administration.

The section on networking fundamentals equips readers with the necessary knowledge to navigate and utilize networks effectively. It highlights the importance of proper network design, scalability, and security considerations. This understanding lays the foundation for exploring internet technologies, network protocols, network administration, and other advanced topics covered in subsequent sections and chapters.

Internet Protocols: TCP/IP, DNS, HTTP, and FTP

The section on "Internet Protocols: TCP/IP, DNS, HTTP, and FTP" in Chapter 4 of "Unleashing the Power of Information and Communication Technology: A Comprehensive Guide" provides readers with a comprehensive understanding of the key protocols that underpin the functioning of the internet.

TCP/IP (Transmission Control Protocol/Internet Protocol):

TCP/IP is the fundamental protocol suite that enables communication and data transfer across the internet. In this subsection, readers gain insights into the TCP/IP protocol stack, which consists of multiple layers, including the network interface layer, internet layer, transport layer, and application layer. Readers learn about the roles of key protocols within the TCP/IP suite, such as IP (Internet Protocol) for addressing and routing, TCP (Transmission Control Protocol) for reliable data delivery, and UDP (User Datagram Protocol) for lightweight and connectionless communication. They also gain an understanding of how TCP/IP allows for the seamless transmission of data packets across networks, ensuring efficient and reliable communication.

DNS (Domain Name System):

The Domain Name System (DNS) plays a crucial role in translating domain names (e.g., www.example.com) into their corresponding IP addresses (e.g., 192.168.0.1). In this subsection, readers learn about the importance of DNS in facilitating human-readable domain names and enabling internet navigation. They gain insights into the DNS hierarchy, including the root servers, top-level domains (TLDs), and authoritative name servers. Readers also learn about the DNS resolution process, where client devices query DNS servers to obtain the IP address associated with a specific domain name.

HTTP (Hypertext Transfer Protocol):

HTTP is the protocol used for transferring hypertext (web) content over the internet. In this subsection, readers gain an understanding of how HTTP facilitates the communication between web clients (such as web browsers) and web servers. They learn about the request-response model of HTTP, where clients send HTTP requests to servers, and servers respond with the requested content. Readers explore different HTTP methods, such as GET, POST, PUT, and DELETE, and their purposes in interacting with web resources. The subsection also covers HTTP headers, status codes, and the importance of secure HTTP (HTTPS) for encrypted communication.

FTP (File Transfer Protocol):

FTP is a protocol that enables the transfer of files between a client and a server over the internet. In this subsection, readers learn about the functionalities of FTP and its applications in file sharing and management. They gain insights into how FTP allows for the uploading and downloading of files, directory listing, and file permission management. The subsection covers the FTP client-server model, where clients establish connections to servers and use FTP commands to interact with remote file systems.

Understanding internet protocols such as TCP/IP, DNS, HTTP, and FTP is crucial for comprehending how data is transmitted, translated, and accessed over the internet. Knowledge of these protocols enables readers to effectively navigate the internet, develop web applications, and troubleshoot network issues. It lays the foundation for exploring advanced topics such as network security, web development, and network administration.

The section on internet protocols equips readers with the necessary knowledge to understand the underlying mechanisms of internet communication. It emphasizes the importance of these protocols in enabling efficient and reliable data transfer, domain name resolution, and web content delivery. This understanding prepares readers for further exploration of internet technologies, network administration, and emerging trends in the field of networking and internet-based applications.

Network Security and Encryption

This section provides readers with a comprehensive understanding of the importance of network security and the role of encryption in safeguarding network communication and data transfer.

Network Security Fundamentals:

This subsection introduces readers to the fundamentals of network security. Readers gain insights into the importance of network security in protecting sensitive information, preventing unauthorized access, and ensuring the confidentiality, integrity, and availability of network resources. They learn about the principles of network security, including authentication, authorization, and accountability. The subsection explores the different types of network security threats, such as malware, hacking, phishing, and denial-of-service attacks.

Firewalls:

Firewalls are essential components of network security that control and monitor network traffic. In this subsection, readers gain an understanding of how firewalls work to filter incoming and outgoing network traffic based on predefined rules. They learn about different types of firewalls, such as packet-filtering firewalls, stateful inspection firewalls, and application-level gateways. Readers also explore the concept of a demilitarized zone (DMZ) and its role in separating public-facing servers from the internal network.

Intrusion Detection Systems (IDS) and Intrusion Prevention Systems (IPS):

Intrusion Detection Systems (IDS) and Intrusion Prevention Systems (IPS) play a crucial role in network security by identifying and responding to malicious activities. This subsection explores IDS and IPS, highlighting their capabilities in detecting and alerting network administrators about potential security breaches. Readers learn about the different types of IDS and IPS, including signature-based and behavior-based systems. They gain insights into the importance of continuous monitoring, event logging, and real-time threat intelligence in maintaining network security.

Virtual Private Networks (VPNs):

Virtual Private Networks (VPNs) provide secure remote access to private networks over the internet. In this subsection, readers gain an understanding of VPNs and their role in establishing secure and encrypted communication between remote users and corporate networks. They learn about the components of a VPN, including VPN protocols (such as IPsec and SSL/TLS), VPN clients, and VPN gateways. Readers also explore the concept of tunneling and how VPNs ensure confidentiality and integrity of data transmitted over public networks.

Encryption:

Encryption is a crucial technique in network security that ensures the confidentiality and integrity of data during transmission. This subsection delves into encryption and its practical applications. Readers learn about symmetric encryption, where the same key is used for both encryption and decryption, and asymmetric encryption, which involves the use of public and private key pairs. They gain insights into encryption algorithms such as AES (Advanced Encryption Standard) and RSA (Rivest-Shamir-Adleman). The subsection also covers the importance of secure key management and digital certificates in encryption.

User Awareness and Best Practices:

This subsection highlights the importance of user awareness and adherence to best practices in maintaining network security. Readers learn about the significance of strong and unique passwords, two-factor authentication, and regular software updates. They gain insights into social engineering attacks and the need for user education and awareness. The subsection emphasizes the importance of security policies, access control, and regular security audits in maintaining a robust network security posture.

Understanding network security and encryption is crucial in protecting network communication and data transfer from unauthorized access and potential threats. Knowledge of network security fundamentals, firewalls, intrusion detection and prevention systems, VPNs, and encryption techniques equips readers with the necessary tools to safeguard network resources. It provides a foundation for exploring advanced network security topics, such as network monitoring, incident response, and security architecture.

The section on network security and encryption underscores the significance of maintaining a proactive and multi-layered approach to network security. It emphasizes the importance of continuous monitoring, regular updates, user education, and adherence to security best practices. This understanding prepares readers to address the evolving landscape of network threats and secure network infrastructures effectively.

Cloud Computing and Virtualization

This section provides readers with a comprehensive understanding of the concepts, benefits, and practical applications of cloud computing and virtualization.

Introduction to Cloud Computing:

This subsection introduces readers to the concept of cloud computing. Readers learn that cloud computing involves the delivery of computing resources, such as servers, storage, databases, and software, over the internet on a pay-as-you-go basis. They gain insights into the key characteristics of cloud computing, including on-demand self-service, broad network access, resource pooling, rapid elasticity, and measured service. The subsection explores different cloud service models, including Infrastructure as a Service (IaaS), Platform as a Service (PaaS), and Software as a Service (SaaS).

Benefits of Cloud Computing:

This subsection highlights the benefits of cloud computing. Readers learn about the scalability and flexibility offered by cloud computing, enabling organizations to rapidly scale their resources based on demand. They gain an understanding of the cost-effectiveness of cloud computing, as organizations can pay for resources on a usage-based model rather than making significant upfront investments. The subsection also explores the reliability, availability, and global accessibility of cloud services. Readers learn about the potential for innovation, collaboration, and improved disaster recovery that cloud computing offers.

Virtualization:

Virtualization is a foundational technology that underlies cloud computing. In this subsection, readers explore virtualization and its role in creating virtual instances of computing resources. They gain insights into server virtualization, where a physical server is partitioned into multiple virtual machines (VMs). Readers also learn about hypervisors, which manage the virtualization layer and enable the efficient utilization of physical resources. The subsection covers the benefits of virtualization, including improved resource utilization, flexibility, and isolation.

Cloud Deployment Models:

This subsection delves into different cloud deployment models. Readers learn about public clouds, where cloud services are available to the general public over the internet. They gain insights into private clouds, which are dedicated to a single organization and provide enhanced control and security. The subsection also explores hybrid clouds, which combine public and private clouds, and community clouds, which serve specific groups or communities with shared requirements. Readers learn about the considerations for selecting the appropriate cloud deployment model based on security, compliance, performance, and cost requirements.

Cloud Security and Governance:

The subsection on cloud security and governance addresses the importance of maintaining security in cloud computing environments. Readers gain insights into the shared responsibility model, where cloud service providers and cloud customers have distinct security responsibilities. They learn about the importance of data protection, encryption, identity and access management, and compliance in cloud environments. The subsection also covers the significance of cloud governance frameworks, service-level agreements (SLAs), and vendor management in ensuring secure and compliant cloud deployments.

Understanding cloud computing and virtualization is essential in harnessing the benefits of scalable, flexible, and cost-effective computing resources. Knowledge of cloud service models, virtualization technologies, deployment models, and security considerations equips readers with the necessary tools to leverage cloud computing in various domains and applications. It provides a foundation for exploring advanced topics such as cloud architecture, cloud-native development, and cloud orchestration.

The section on cloud computing and virtualization highlights the transformative nature of cloud technologies in modern computing. It emphasizes the potential for innovation, agility, and cost savings that cloud computing offers. This understanding prepares readers to embrace cloud technologies, architect cloud solutions, and effectively manage cloud environments for improved productivity and business outcomes.

CHAPTER 5: WEB TECHNOLOGIES

This chapter provides readers with a comprehensive understanding of website design and development, HTML, CSS, JavaScript, content management systems (CMS), and web services and APIs.

Website Design and Development

This section provides readers with a comprehensive understanding of the process and principles involved in creating effective and engaging websites.

User-Centric Design:

User-centric design is at the core of website development. In this subsection, readers learn about the importance of understanding user needs, behaviors, and expectations. They gain insights into techniques such as user research, personas, and user journey mapping, which help in creating user-centered websites. The subsection emphasizes the significance of usability and accessibility considerations to ensure that websites are intuitive, easy to navigate, and inclusive for all users.

Website Development Process:

The website development process involves several stages. Readers are introduced to the different stages, including requirements gathering, wireframing, prototyping, visual design, and front-end and back-end development. They learn about the significance of establishing clear goals, understanding client or user requirements, and creating effective project timelines. The subsection emphasizes the importance of collaboration among web designers, developers, and stakeholders throughout the development process.

Responsive Design:

Responsive design is a crucial aspect of modern website development. Readers gain an understanding of responsive design principles, which ensure that websites adapt and provide optimal user experiences across various devices and screen sizes. They learn about the use of media queries, flexible grids, and responsive images to achieve responsiveness. The subsection also explores the importance of mobile-first design and the impact of responsive design on search engine optimization (SEO) and user engagement.

Search Engine Optimization (SEO):

Search Engine Optimization (SEO) plays a vital role in website development. Readers learn about SEO techniques and best practices to improve the visibility and ranking of websites in search engine results. They gain insights into on-page SEO factors such as keyword research, meta tags, URL structure, and content optimization. Readers also explore off-page SEO strategies, including link building and social media presence. The subsection highlights the importance of creating SEO-friendly websites that are easily discoverable and accessible to search engines.

Website Performance Optimization:

Website performance optimization is crucial for delivering a fast and seamless user experience. In this subsection, readers learn about techniques to optimize website performance, including optimizing images, minifying code, leveraging caching, and reducing server response time. They gain insights into the use of performance monitoring tools and techniques to identify bottlenecks and improve overall website performance. The subsection also covers the importance of web hosting selection and content delivery networks (CDNs) for enhancing website speed and performance.

Understanding website design and development principles is essential for creating visually appealing, user-friendly, and high-performing websites. Knowledge of user-centric design, the website development process, responsive design, SEO, and performance optimization equips readers with the necessary tools to design and build websites that meet user needs and business objectives. It lays the foundation for exploring advanced web development concepts, such as front-end frameworks, back-end programming languages, content management systems, and web accessibility.

The section on website design and development emphasizes the importance of delivering exceptional user experiences through well-designed and optimized websites. It highlights the significance of aligning design, functionality, and performance to create websites that engage users, achieve business goals, and leave a lasting impression. This understanding prepares readers to create impactful and successful web experiences in today's digital landscape.

HTML, CSS, and JavaScript

HTML, CSS, and JavaScript are three fundamental technologies in web development. They work together to create interactive, visually appealing, and dynamic web pages. The section on "HTML, CSS, and JavaScript" in Chapter 5 of "Unleashing the Power of Information and Communication Technology: A Comprehensive Guide" provides readers with a comprehensive understanding of these technologies and their roles in web development.

HTML (Hypertext Markup Language):

HTML is the standard markup language used to structure and present content on the web. In this subsection, readers learn about the basic elements, tags, and attributes of HTML. They gain insights into the semantic elements introduced in HTML5, which provide meaning and structure to web content. Readers also explore the importance of accessibility in HTML, including the use of alt attributes for images and the proper semantic structure of web pages. The subsection emphasizes the significance of clean, well-structured HTML code for search engine optimization and web accessibility.

CSS (Cascading Style Sheets):

CSS is used to control the visual appearance and layout of web pages. Readers gain an understanding of CSS and its role in styling HTML elements. They learn about CSS selectors, properties, and values, which allow for precise control over the presentation of web content. Readers also explore box model concepts, including margins, borders, padding, and the use of positioning and floating to create flexible layouts. The subsection highlights the importance of CSS in achieving responsive design and consistent branding across web pages.

JavaScript:

JavaScript is a powerful scripting language that adds interactivity and dynamic behavior to web pages. In this subsection, readers gain an understanding of JavaScript and its role in web development. They learn about variables, data types, operators, control structures, and functions in JavaScript. Readers explore the manipulation of the Document Object Model (DOM) using JavaScript, allowing for the dynamic update and manipulation of web page elements. They also gain insights into event handling, form validation, and asynchronous programming using JavaScript. The subsection highlights the importance of JavaScript in creating interactive web experiences, handling user input, and facilitating client-side interactions.

Understanding HTML, CSS, and JavaScript is essential for web development. Knowledge of these technologies enables readers to structure web content, control its visual presentation, and add interactivity to web pages. It provides a foundation for creating user-friendly, visually appealing, and responsive websites. Additionally, understanding the interactions between HTML, CSS, and JavaScript is crucial for effective collaboration between web designers and developers.

The section on HTML, CSS, and JavaScript emphasizes the significance of mastering these core web technologies. It highlights the importance of writing clean and well-structured code, adhering to web standards, and following best practices. This understanding prepares readers to create modern, dynamic, and interactive web pages that engage users and deliver exceptional web experiences.

Content Management Systems (CMS)

Content Management Systems (CMS) have revolutionized the way websites are created, managed, and updated. This section provides readers with a comprehensive understanding of CMS platforms and their role in website development and content management.

Introduction to Content Management Systems:

This subsection introduces readers to Content Management Systems (CMS) and their significance in web development. Readers gain insights into the purpose of CMS platforms, which is to simplify the creation, organization, and publication of digital content. They learn about the advantages of using CMS for website development, including the ability to manage content without technical expertise, the separation of content from design, and the facilitation of collaboration among multiple content contributors. The subsection also explores the history and evolution of CMS platforms.

Popular CMS Platforms:

Readers are introduced to popular CMS platforms used in website development. They gain insights into platforms such as WordPress, Joomla, Drupal, and others. Readers learn about the features and capabilities of these CMS platforms, including content creation, management, customization, and extensions. The subsection explores the availability of themes and templates, which allow for the customization of website design. Readers also gain an understanding of the community support, plugins, and ecosystem surrounding these CMS platforms.

Content Creation and Management:

This subsection delves into content creation and management in CMS platforms. Readers learn about the user-friendly interfaces provided by CMS platforms, which simplify the process of creating and editing content. They gain insights into content organization, including the use of categories, tags, and taxonomies to enhance the structure and discoverability of content. The subsection explores features such as version control, workflow management, and user roles, which enable efficient content management and collaboration among content contributors.

Customization and Themes:

Readers learn about the customization capabilities of CMS platforms. They gain insights into the use of themes and templates to change the visual design of websites. The subsection explores the availability of pre-built themes and the ability to create custom themes to match specific branding requirements. Readers also learn about the importance of responsive design in selecting and customizing themes for optimal viewing across devices.

Plugins and Extensions:

CMS platforms offer a wide range of plugins and extensions that enhance the functionality of websites. In this subsection, readers explore the availability of plugins for various purposes, such as e-commerce, SEO, social media integration, and forms. They learn about the process of installing and configuring plugins to extend the features and capabilities of CMS platforms. Readers also gain insights into the importance of selecting reliable and regularly maintained plugins for security and compatibility.

Security and Updates:

Security is a critical aspect of CMS platforms. This subsection highlights the importance of keeping CMS platforms and plugins up to date to address security vulnerabilities. Readers learn about best practices for securing CMS installations, including the use of strong passwords, regular backups, and the implementation of security plugins. The subsection emphasizes the significance of maintaining a proactive approach to security to protect websites and their content from potential threats.

Understanding Content Management Systems (CMS) is essential for efficient website development and content management. Knowledge of CMS platforms, content creation and management, customization, plugins, and security equips readers with the necessary tools to leverage CMS platforms effectively. It provides a foundation for creating, managing, and maintaining websites with ease and scalability.

The section on Content Management Systems (CMS) emphasizes the transformative role of CMS platforms in simplifying website development and content management. It highlights the benefits of using CMS, such as increased productivity, collaboration, and flexibility. This understanding prepares readers to make informed decisions regarding the selection, implementation, and customization of CMS platforms for their website development projects.

Web Services and APIs

Web Services and APIs (Application Programming Interfaces) play a crucial role in enabling seamless communication and data exchange between different systems and applications. The section on "Web Services and APIs" in Chapter 5 of "Unleashing the Power of Information and Communication Technology: A Comprehensive Guide" provides readers with a comprehensive understanding of these technologies and their practical applications.

Introduction to Web Services and APIs:

This subsection introduces readers to the concept of web services and APIs. Readers gain insights into how web services enable interoperability between different systems and applications over the internet. They learn about the role of APIs in defining the rules and protocols for communication and data exchange. The subsection emphasizes the importance of standardization and adherence to industry-accepted API specifications for seamless integration between systems.

Representational State Transfer (REST):

Representational State Transfer (REST) is a widely used architectural style for web services. In this subsection, readers learn about RESTful web services and their key principles, including statelessness, resource-based interactions, and the use of HTTP methods (GET, POST, PUT, DELETE) to perform operations on resources. They gain insights into the importance of well-defined API endpoints, request and response formats (such as JSON or XML), and status codes for effective communication between client and server.

API Documentation and Design:

API documentation plays a critical role in facilitating the integration and use of APIs. Readers gain an understanding of the importance of comprehensive and well-documented APIs. They explore best practices for API documentation, including clear and concise descriptions of endpoints, request parameters, response formats, and authentication requirements. The subsection also covers the significance of API design, including versioning, error handling, and naming conventions, to ensure consistency and ease of use for API consumers.

Authentication and Authorization:

Authentication and authorization are vital aspects of API security. In this subsection, readers learn about different authentication mechanisms used in APIs, such as API keys, OAuth, and JSON Web Tokens (JWT). They gain insights into the importance of securing API endpoints and limiting access to authorized users or applications. The subsection explores the use of access control mechanisms, such as role-based access control (RBAC), to enforce granular permissions and protect sensitive data.

Practical Applications of Web Services and APIs:

This subsection highlights the practical applications of web services and APIs in various domains. Readers explore the use of APIs for integrating social media platforms, payment gateways, mapping services, weather data, and many other functionalities into web applications. They gain insights into the potential of API ecosystems and third-party integrations to enhance the capabilities and reach of web applications. The subsection also covers emerging trends, such as the Internet of Things (IoT) and microservices, and their impact on web service architectures.

Understanding web services and APIs is essential for building interconnected and efficient systems. Knowledge of RESTful principles, API documentation, authentication, and practical applications enables readers to effectively integrate APIs into their web applications. It provides a foundation for creating scalable, modular, and interoperable systems that leverage the capabilities of external services.

The section on web services and APIs emphasizes the significance of standardization, documentation, and security in API design and usage. It highlights the transformative potential of APIs in enabling seamless data exchange and system integration. This understanding prepares readers to harness the power of web services and APIs in their web development projects and stay up to date with the evolving landscape of interconnected systems.

CHAPTER 6: DATABASE SYSTEMS

This chapter provides readers with a comprehensive understanding of databases, relational database management systems (RDBMS), Structured Query Language (SQL), and database design and normalization.

Introduction to Databases

This section provides readers with a comprehensive understanding of databases and their significance in information management.

Purpose of Databases:

The subsection begins by introducing readers to the purpose of databases. Databases serve as central repositories for storing, organizing, and managing structured data. They provide a systematic way to store large volumes of data and enable efficient retrieval and manipulation of that data. Readers learn that databases are essential for managing various types of information, such as customer records, product inventories, financial transactions, and more.

Advantages of Databases:

Readers gain insights into the advantages of using databases over traditional file-based systems. Databases offer several benefits, including improved data consistency, as data is stored in a centralized location and follows predefined rules. They ensure data integrity by enforcing constraints and validation rules. Additionally, databases provide better data security through access control mechanisms, allowing authorized users to access and modify data. The subsection also explores the advantages of data sharing and data independence in databases.

Types of Databases:

This subsection explores different types of databases. Readers learn about hierarchical databases, where data is organized in a tree-like structure, with parent-child relationships. They gain insights into network databases, which allow for complex relationships and multiple parent-child connections. The subsection also introduces object-oriented databases, which store data as objects with attributes and behaviors. Lastly, readers are introduced to relational databases, the most widely used type, where data is organized into tables with rows and columns, linked through keys and relationships.

Relational Database Concepts:

Readers delve into the core concepts of relational databases. They learn about entities, which represent real-world objects or concepts, and attributes, which describe characteristics of entities. Relationships between entities are explored, including one-to-one, one-to-many, and many-to-many relationships. Readers also gain insights into keys, such as primary keys and foreign keys, which ensure data integrity and establish relationships between tables.

Data Manipulation Language (DML) and Data Definition Language (DDL):

The subsection introduces readers to Data Manipulation Language (DML) and Data Definition Language (DDL). DML allows for the retrieval, insertion, modification, and deletion of data in databases. Readers learn about SQL (Structured Query Language), the standard language for interacting with relational databases. DDL, on the other hand, focuses on defining and modifying the structure of the database. It includes commands to create, alter, and delete tables, indexes, and other database objects.

Understanding databases is crucial for efficient data management and retrieval. Knowledge of the purpose of databases, their advantages over file-based systems, and the different types of databases equips readers with a solid foundation in information management. It provides a basis for exploring advanced topics in database design, query optimization, and database administration.

The section on Introduction to Databases emphasizes the significance of databases as central repositories for managing structured data. It highlights the advantages of databases in ensuring data consistency, integrity, and security. This understanding prepares readers to work with databases effectively, design database systems, and make informed decisions regarding data storage and retrieval for various applications and industries.

Relational Database Management Systems (RDBMS)

Relational Database Management Systems (RDBMS) are widely used in modern data management systems. This section provides readers with a comprehensive understanding of RDBMS and their significance in data storage and retrieval.

Relational Model:

The subsection begins by introducing readers to the relational model, which forms the foundation of RDBMS. Readers gain insights into the key principles of the relational model, including the organization of data into tables, the representation of relationships between tables, and the use of keys to establish and enforce data integrity.

They learn that the relational model provides a logical and structured approach to organizing and managing data.

Tables, Rows, and Columns:

Readers explore the fundamental components of RDBMS, namely tables, rows, and columns. Tables are used to store data in a structured manner. Each table consists of rows, also known as records or tuples, which represent individual instances of data, and columns, which define the attributes or properties of the data. Readers gain an understanding of how tables, rows, and columns are interconnected to form a relational database.

Entities, Relationships, and Keys:

Entities and relationships are crucial concepts in RDBMS. Readers learn that entities represent real-world objects or concepts, such as customers, products, or employees. Relationships define the associations between entities, such as a customer placing an order or an employee belonging to a department. They gain insights into different types of relationships, including one-to-one, one-to-many, and many-to-many relationships. Keys, such as primary keys and foreign keys, are explored, as they are used to uniquely identify and establish relationships between entities.

Data Integrity and Constraints:

Data integrity is a critical aspect of RDBMS. The subsection explores the importance of maintaining data integrity to ensure the accuracy and consistency of data. Readers learn about various types of constraints, such as primary key constraints, foreign key constraints, and uniqueness constraints, which enforce rules and restrictions on the data. They gain insights into the role of constraints in preventing duplicate data, maintaining referential integrity, and preserving the validity of relationships.

Normalization:

Normalization is an essential process in database design that reduces redundancy and ensures data integrity. Readers delve into the concept of normalization and its importance in RDBMS. They learn about the different normal forms, such as First Normal Form (1NF), Second Normal Form (2NF), and Third Normal Form (3NF). Readers gain insights into the steps involved in the normalization process, including identifying functional dependencies and removing data anomalies through table restructuring.

SQL and RDBMS Operations:

Structured Query Language (SQL) is the standard language for interacting with RDBMS. Readers explore SQL and its role in performing various operations on relational databases. They gain an understanding of SQL commands for data retrieval (SELECT), data insertion (INSERT), data modification (UPDATE), and data deletion (DELETE). The subsection highlights the significance of SQL in querying and manipulating data in RDBMS.

Understanding Relational Database Management Systems (RDBMS) is crucial for effective data storage, organization, and retrieval. Knowledge of the relational model, tables, rows, columns, entities, relationships, data integrity, normalization, and SQL equips readers with the necessary tools to design, query, and maintain relational databases. It provides a foundation for building scalable, efficient, and secure data management systems.

The section on Relational Database Management Systems (RDBMS) emphasizes the significance of the relational model and its principles in modern data management. It highlights the importance of data integrity, normalization, and SQL in effective database design and operations. This understanding prepares readers to work with RDBMS effectively and make informed decisions regarding data storage, organization, and retrieval in various domains and applications.

Structured Query Language (SQL)

Structured Query Language (SQL) is a standard language for interacting with relational databases. It provides a powerful set of commands and syntax for managing data, querying databases, and performing various operations. This section provides readers with a comprehensive understanding of SQL and its significance in database management.

Basic SQL Commands:

The subsection begins by introducing readers to the basic SQL commands. Readers learn about the SELECT command, which is used to retrieve data from one or more tables in a database. They gain insights into the INSERT command for adding new records to a table, the UPDATE command for modifying existing records, and the DELETE command for removing records from a table. The subsection emphasizes the importance of understanding the syntax and proper usage of these commands to perform data manipulation effectively.

Data Querying with SQL:

SQL is widely used for querying databases to extract specific information. Readers gain an understanding of the SELECT statement, which allows for precise data retrieval based on specified conditions. They explore various clauses in the SELECT statement, such as WHERE, ORDER BY, GROUP BY, and HAVING, which enable filtering, sorting, grouping, and aggregating data. The subsection also covers the use of SQL functions for performing calculations, string manipulation, date and time operations, and more.

Joins and Subqueries:

Joining tables is a fundamental concept in SQL to combine data from multiple tables based on common columns. Readers delve into different types of joins, including inner joins, outer joins (left join, right join, and full outer join), and self-joins. They gain insights into using subqueries, which are nested queries within a larger query, to retrieve data based on results from other queries. The subsection explores the use of joins and subqueries to retrieve complex and meaningful information from relational databases.

Data Manipulation with SQL:

SQL provides powerful commands for data manipulation in databases. Readers learn about the INSERT statement and its various forms for inserting data into tables. They gain insights into the UPDATE statement for modifying existing records, including updating specific columns or updating records based on specified conditions. The subsection also covers the DELETE statement for removing records from tables. Readers explore the importance of proper usage and caution when executing data manipulation commands to maintain data integrity.

Database Creation and Modification with SQL:

SQL facilitates the creation and modification of database objects. Readers gain an understanding of the CREATE statement for creating databases, tables, indexes, and other database objects. They explore the ALTER statement for modifying existing database objects, such as adding or dropping columns or constraints. The subsection also covers the DROP statement for deleting database objects. Readers learn about the importance of properly structuring and managing database objects through SQL commands.

SQL and Database Administration:

Database administration involves managing and maintaining databases effectively. The subsection highlights the role of SQL in database administration tasks. Readers learn about creating and managing user accounts, granting and revoking permissions, and enforcing access control through SQL statements. They gain insights into the importance of SQL for database backup and recovery, performance tuning, and monitoring database activity.

Understanding Structured Query Language (SQL) is essential for effective database management and data retrieval. Knowledge of SQL commands, data querying, joins, subqueries, data manipulation, database creation and modification, and database administration equips readers with the necessary tools to interact with relational databases. It provides a foundation for building efficient, secure, and scalable data management systems.

The section on Structured Query Language (SQL) emphasizes the significance of SQL in managing and manipulating data in relational databases. It highlights the importance of understanding SQL syntax, proper usage of SQL commands, and best practices for efficient data retrieval and manipulation. This understanding prepares readers to work with SQL effectively, design complex queries, and maintain databases in various domains and applications.

Database Design and Normalization

This section focuses on the essential concepts and techniques involved in designing well-structured databases and achieving data normalization.

Importance of Database Design:

The subsection begins by emphasizing the significance of database design in creating efficient and effective databases. Readers learn that proper database design ensures data integrity, minimizes redundancy, and maximizes the efficiency of data retrieval and manipulation. They understand that a well-designed database is scalable, adaptable, and facilitates accurate and meaningful data analysis.

Entity-Relationship (ER) Modeling:

ER modeling is a widely used technique for designing databases. Readers explore the concept of entities, which represent real-world objects or concepts, and relationships, which define associations between entities. They gain insights into the various types of relationships, including one-to-one, one-to-many, and many-to-many relationships. The subsection highlights the importance of identifying entities, attributes, and relationships in the early stages of database design.

Database Normalization:

Normalization is a crucial process in database design that reduces redundancy and ensures data integrity. Readers delve into the concept of normalization and its significance in creating well-structured databases. They gain an understanding of the different normal forms, such as First Normal Form (1NF), Second Normal Form (2NF), and Third Normal Form (3NF). The subsection explains the step-by-step process of normalization, which involves identifying functional dependencies and restructuring tables to eliminate data anomalies.

First Normal Form (1NF):

The subsection explores the concept of First Normal Form (1NF), which sets the foundation for database normalization. Readers learn that 1NF requires eliminating repeating groups and ensuring atomicity of data by organizing data into individual columns within a table. They gain insights into the importance of unique identifiers (primary keys) to uniquely identify each record in a table.

Second Normal Form (2NF):

Readers delve into the concept of Second Normal Form (2NF), which builds upon the principles of 1NF. They learn that 2NF requires eliminating partial dependencies, where attributes depend on only a part of the primary key. The subsection explores the process of identifying and separating data into separate tables to achieve 2NF. Readers gain insights into the significance of foreign keys to establish relationships between related tables.

Third Normal Form (3NF):

The subsection introduces readers to Third Normal Form (3NF), which further refines the database design. Readers learn that 3NF requires eliminating transitive dependencies, where attributes depend on other non-key attributes. They explore the process of identifying and eliminating such dependencies by organizing data into separate tables and establishing appropriate relationships. Readers gain insights into the benefits of achieving 3NF, including improved data integrity and reduced redundancy.

Understanding database design and normalization is crucial for creating efficient, scalable, and well-structured databases. Knowledge of ER modeling, normalization concepts, and the step-by-step process of achieving 1NF, 2NF, and 3NF equips readers with the necessary tools to design databases that meet the needs of various applications and domains.

The section on Database Design and Normalization emphasizes the significance of proper database design and normalization techniques. It highlights the importance of eliminating redundancy, ensuring data integrity, and optimizing data retrieval and manipulation. This understanding prepares readers to design databases that are scalable, efficient, and adaptable to evolving business requirements and data management challenges.

CHAPTER 7: INFORMATION SYSTEMS AND ENTERPRISE APPLICATIONS

This chapter focuses on information systems and enterprise application and provides readers with a comprehensive understanding of various enterprise applications and their significance in managing business operations and driving decision-making processes.

Enterprise Resource Planning (ERP)

Enterprise Resource Planning (ERP) systems play a crucial role in integrating and streamlining business processes across various departments and functions within an organization. This section provides readers with a comprehensive understanding of ERP systems and their significance in managing business operations.

Introduction to ERP:

The subsection begins by introducing readers to the concept of ERP systems. Readers gain insights into the purpose of ERP systems, which is to provide a centralized and integrated platform for managing and automating various business functions. They learn that ERP systems enable organizations to streamline processes, improve operational efficiency, enhance data visibility, and facilitate informed decision-making. The subsection explores the evolution of ERP systems and their adoption across diverse industries.

ERP Modules and Functionalities:

ERP systems consist of various modules that cater to different business functions within an organization. Readers delve into the core modules commonly found in ERP systems, such as finance and accounting, human resources, supply chain management, inventory management, sales and marketing, and customer relationship management. They gain an understanding of how these modules interact and share data, enabling seamless information flow across departments. The subsection emphasizes the benefits of having a unified ERP system for eliminating data silos and achieving process efficiency.

Benefits of ERP Implementation:

Readers explore the numerous benefits associated with ERP implementation. They learn that ERP systems provide real-time and accurate data, enabling organizations to make informed decisions based on up-to-date information. ERP systems improve operational efficiency by automating manual tasks, reducing errors, and streamlining workflows. They also enhance collaboration and communication across departments, fostering a cohesive and integrated work environment. The subsection highlights the significance of ERP in improving customer service, reducing costs, and enabling scalability and growth.

ERP Implementation Challenges and Best Practices:

Implementing an ERP system can present challenges and complexities. The subsection discusses common challenges faced during ERP implementation, such as resistance to change, data migration, system integration, and user adoption. Readers gain insights into best practices for successful ERP implementation, including thorough planning and preparation, effective change management strategies, strong executive sponsorship, and user training and support. The subsection emphasizes the importance of selecting the right ERP vendor and aligning the system with organizational goals and requirements.

ERP Trends and Future Developments:

The subsection provides an overview of emerging trends and future developments in the field of ERP. Readers explore topics such as cloud-based ERP systems, mobile accessibility, artificial intelligence (AI) and machine learning (ML) integration, and Internet of Things (IoT) connectivity. They gain insights into the potential of these advancements to further enhance the capabilities and effectiveness of ERP systems. The subsection emphasizes the need for organizations to stay updated with evolving ERP trends to remain competitive in the digital age.

Understanding Enterprise Resource Planning (ERP) is essential for optimizing business operations and achieving operational efficiency. Knowledge of ERP systems, their modules, functionalities, benefits, implementation challenges, and future trends equips readers with the necessary tools to leverage ERP systems effectively. It provides a foundation for successfully implementing and utilizing ERP systems to streamline processes, improve data visibility, and drive organizational growth.

The section on Enterprise Resource Planning (ERP) emphasizes the transformative impact of ERP systems in integrating and optimizing business processes. It highlights the benefits of ERP implementation in achieving operational excellence, data-driven decision-making, and enhanced collaboration. This understanding prepares readers to effectively utilize ERP systems and leverage their capabilities to drive organizational success in today's dynamic and competitive business landscape.

Customer Relationship Management (CRM)

Customer Relationship Management (CRM) systems are essential tools for businesses to effectively manage and nurture relationships with their customers. The section on "Customer Relationship Management (CRM)" in Chapter 7 of "Unleashing the Power of Information and Communication Technology: A Comprehensive Guide" provides readers with a comprehensive understanding of CRM systems and their significance in building strong customer relationships.

Introduction to CRM:

The subsection begins by introducing readers to the concept of CRM systems. Readers gain insights into the purpose of CRM, which is to help organizations manage interactions and relationships with their customers. They learn that CRM systems provide a centralized platform for capturing and organizing customer data, tracking customer interactions, and providing personalized customer experiences. The subsection explores the evolution of CRM systems and their adoption across various industries.

Key Components of CRM:

CRM systems consist of several key components that enable businesses to effectively manage customer relationships. Readers delve into these components, which include:

Contact Management: CRM systems allow businesses to store and organize customer contact information, such as names, addresses, emails, and phone numbers. Contact management functionalities enable businesses to maintain up-to-date and accurate customer records.

Sales Force Automation: CRM systems assist sales teams in managing the sales process. They provide tools for tracking leads, managing opportunities, forecasting sales, and monitoring sales performance. Sales force automation functionalities streamline the sales cycle and improve sales team efficiency.

Customer Service and Support: CRM systems help businesses provide excellent customer service by enabling efficient management of customer inquiries, complaints, and support tickets. They allow businesses to track customer issues, assign tasks, and ensure timely resolution, leading to enhanced customer satisfaction.

Marketing Automation: CRM systems support marketing efforts by automating various marketing activities. These functionalities include lead management, campaign management, email marketing, and customer segmentation. Marketing automation capabilities enable businesses to target the right audience, deliver personalized messages, and measure marketing effectiveness.

Benefits of CRM Implementation:

Readers explore the numerous benefits associated with CRM implementation. They learn that CRM systems help businesses improve customer satisfaction and loyalty by providing personalized experiences based on customer data. CRM systems enable businesses to gain a comprehensive view of their customers, allowing for targeted marketing campaigns and cross-selling or upselling opportunities. They also enhance customer retention by facilitating effective customer service and support. The subsection emphasizes the importance of CRM in driving customer-centric strategies and achieving a competitive advantage.

CRM Integration and Data Analytics:

Integration with other systems and data analytics capabilities are crucial aspects of CRM systems. Readers gain an understanding of how CRM systems integrate with other business applications, such as ERP systems or marketing automation tools, to ensure seamless data flow across departments. They explore the importance of data analytics in CRM, as it allows businesses to derive insights from customer data, identify trends and patterns, and make data-driven decisions. The subsection highlights the significance of leveraging analytics to optimize marketing campaigns, improve customer segmentation, and drive business growth.

CRM Implementation Challenges and Best Practices:

Implementing a CRM system can present challenges, and the subsection discusses common challenges faced during CRM implementation, such as data quality issues, user adoption, and system customization. Readers gain insights into best practices for successful CRM implementation, including clearly defining goals and objectives, involving key stakeholders, aligning CRM strategy with business objectives, and providing adequate user training and support. The subsection emphasizes the importance of selecting the right CRM vendor and tailoring the system to meet specific business needs.

Understanding Customer Relationship Management (CRM) is crucial for businesses to effectively manage customer interactions and foster strong relationships. Knowledge of

CRM systems, their key components, benefits, integration with other systems, data analytics capabilities, and implementation best practices equips readers with the necessary tools to leverage CRM effectively. It provides a foundation for successfully implementing and utilizing CRM systems to enhance customer satisfaction, drive sales, and improve overall business performance.

The section on Customer Relationship Management (CRM) emphasizes the transformative impact of CRM systems in managing and nurturing customer relationships. It highlights the benefits of CRM implementation in achieving customer-centric strategies, improving marketing effectiveness, and enhancing customer loyalty. This understanding prepares readers to effectively utilize CRM systems and leverage their capabilities to drive customer satisfaction and long-term business success in today's competitive marketplace.

Business Intelligence (BI) and Data Analytics

Business Intelligence (BI) and Data Analytics play a vital role in helping organizations make informed decisions and gain valuable insights from their data. The section on "Business Intelligence and Data Analytics" in Chapter 7 of "Unleashing the Power of Information and Communication Technology: A Comprehensive Guide" provides readers with a comprehensive understanding of BI and data analytics and their significance in driving business success.

Introduction to Business Intelligence:

The subsection begins by introducing readers to the concept of Business Intelligence. Readers gain insights into the purpose of BI, which is to transform raw data into meaningful insights for informed decision-making. They learn that BI encompasses various tools, techniques, and processes that enable organizations to collect, analyze, and visualize data from different sources. The subsection explores the evolution of BI and its adoption across diverse industries.

Data Management and Integration:

Effective BI requires robust data management and integration processes. Readers delve into the importance of data quality, data integration, and data governance in ensuring accurate and reliable data for analysis. They gain insights into the challenges associated with data management, such as data silos, data inconsistencies, and data privacy concerns. The subsection emphasizes the significance of establishing a solid data foundation to support BI initiatives.

Data Analysis Techniques:

Readers explore different data analysis techniques used in BI and data analytics. They gain an understanding of descriptive analytics, which involves analyzing historical data to gain insights into past performance. They also delve into diagnostic analytics, which focuses on understanding the causes of past events. Furthermore, readers learn about predictive analytics, which uses statistical models and machine learning algorithms to forecast future outcomes. The subsection highlights the importance of selecting appropriate analysis techniques based on the organization's objectives and available data.

Data Visualization and Reporting:

Data visualization is a critical aspect of BI and data analytics. Readers learn about the significance of presenting data in a visual and interactive format to facilitate understanding and interpretation. They explore various data visualization techniques, including charts, graphs, dashboards, and heatmaps. The subsection emphasizes the importance of creating clear and compelling visualizations to communicate insights effectively. Readers also gain insights into reporting capabilities, including automated reporting and ad-hoc reporting, to share data-driven insights with stakeholders.

Data-driven Decision Making:

BI and data analytics enable data-driven decision-making processes within organizations. Readers explore the significance of using data and insights to guide strategic, operational, and tactical decisions. They gain insights into the benefits of data-driven decision-making, including improved accuracy, reduced uncertainty, and increased operational efficiency. The subsection emphasizes the importance of fostering a data-driven culture and providing the necessary tools and training to empower employees to make data-informed decisions.

Emerging Trends in BI and Data Analytics:

The subsection provides an overview of emerging trends and future developments in the field of BI and data analytics. Readers explore topics such as advanced analytics, machine learning, artificial intelligence, and natural language processing. They gain insights into the potential of these advancements to further enhance the capabilities and effectiveness of BI and data analytics. The subsection highlights the importance of staying updated with emerging trends to leverage the full potential of data for strategic advantage.

Understanding Business Intelligence and Data Analytics is crucial for organizations to extract meaningful insights from their data and make informed decisions. Knowledge of BI concepts, data management, analysis techniques, data visualization, and data-driven decision-making equips readers with the necessary tools to leverage data effectively. It provides a foundation for implementing robust BI strategies and utilizing data analytics to drive organizational growth and competitiveness.

The section on Business Intelligence and Data Analytics emphasizes the transformative impact of leveraging data for decision-making. It highlights the benefits of BI and data analytics in gaining valuable insights, improving operational efficiency, and driving innovation. This understanding prepares readers to effectively utilize BI and data analytics tools and techniques to extract actionable insights and foster data-driven decision-making within their organizations.

E-commerce and Online Payment Systems

E-commerce and online payment systems have revolutionized the way businesses operate and customers engage in transactions. The section on "E-commerce and Online Payment Systems" in Chapter 7 of "Unleashing the Power of Information and Communication Technology: A Comprehensive Guide" provides readers with a comprehensive understanding of e-commerce and the significance of online payment systems in facilitating secure and convenient online transactions.

Introduction to E-commerce:

The subsection begins by introducing readers to the concept of e-commerce. Readers gain insights into the purpose of e-commerce, which is the buying and selling of products and services over the internet. They learn about the various types of e-commerce models, including Business-to-Consumer (B2C), Business-to-Business (B2B), Consumer-to-Consumer (C2C), and Mobile Commerce (m-commerce). The subsection explores the growth and impact of e-commerce on industries and consumer behavior.

E-commerce Infrastructure:

Readers delve into the essential components of an e-commerce infrastructure. They explore the significance of having a user-friendly and visually appealing online storefront or website. They learn about the importance of product catalogs, search functionality, and shopping carts in providing a seamless shopping experience. The subsection also covers the importance of secure and reliable hosting, data storage, and website performance in supporting e-commerce operations.

Online Payment Systems:

The subsection introduces readers to the critical role of online payment systems in facilitating secure and convenient transactions in e-commerce. They gain insights into the importance of offering multiple payment options to customers, including credit cards, debit cards, digital wallets, and online banking. Readers explore the significance of integrating secure payment gateways into e-commerce platforms to ensure the safe transfer of sensitive financial information. The subsection emphasizes the importance of trust and security in online payment systems to build customer confidence.

Payment Gateway Integration:

Readers delve into the process of integrating payment gateways with e-commerce platforms. They gain an understanding of how payment gateways enable the encryption and transmission of customer payment information securely. They learn about the role of APIs (Application Programming Interfaces) in facilitating seamless communication between e-commerce platforms and payment gateways. The subsection highlights the importance of selecting reliable and trusted payment gateways that comply with industry standards and regulations.

Security and Fraud Prevention:

Security is a critical aspect of e-commerce and online payment systems. Readers explore the various security measures and fraud prevention techniques employed to protect customer information and prevent unauthorized transactions. They gain insights into the importance of Secure Socket Layer (SSL) encryption, tokenization, and two-factor authentication in ensuring data security. The subsection emphasizes the significance of complying with Payment Card Industry Data Security Standard (PCI DSS) requirements to maintain a secure payment environment.

Emerging Trends in E-commerce and Online Payments:

The subsection provides an overview of emerging trends and future developments in the field of e-commerce and online payment systems. Readers explore topics such as mobile commerce, voice commerce, omnichannel integration, and blockchain technology. They gain insights into the potential of these advancements to enhance the customer experience, improve payment security, and enable innovative business models. The subsection highlights the importance of staying updated with emerging trends to remain competitive in the rapidly evolving e-commerce landscape.

Understanding E-commerce and Online Payment Systems is crucial for businesses to engage in digital commerce and facilitate secure online transactions. Knowledge of e-commerce models, infrastructure components, online payment systems, payment gateway integration, security measures, and emerging trends equips readers with the necessary tools to establish and optimize e-commerce operations. It provides a foundation for implementing secure and user-friendly online payment systems that cater to the evolving needs of customers.

The section on E-commerce and Online Payment Systems emphasizes the transformative impact of digital commerce and the significance of secure payment systems. It highlights the benefits of e-commerce in expanding market reach, improving customer convenience, and driving business growth. This understanding prepares readers to effectively leverage e-commerce and online payment systems to establish a strong online presence, attract and retain customers, and achieve success in the digital marketplace.

CHAPTER 8: EMERGING TECHNOLOGIES

This chapter focuses on emerging technologies that are shaping the future of various industries. This chapter provides readers with a comprehensive understanding of various emerging technologies.

Artificial Intelligence (AI) and Machine Learning

Artificial Intelligence (AI) and Machine Learning are revolutionizing various industries by enabling machines to perform tasks that traditionally required human intelligence. This section provides readers with a comprehensive understanding of AI and machine learning and their transformative potential.

Introduction to Artificial Intelligence (AI):

The subsection begins by introducing readers to the concept of Artificial Intelligence. Readers gain insights into the purpose of AI, which is to develop intelligent systems that can mimic human intelligence and perform tasks autonomously. They learn about the different types of AI, including narrow AI (focused on specific tasks) and general AI (possessing human-like intelligence). The subsection explores the historical background of AI, its evolution, and the advancements made in recent years.

Machine Learning:

Readers delve into the concept of Machine Learning, a subset of AI that focuses on the development of algorithms and models that can learn from data and improve performance over time. They gain an understanding of supervised learning, unsupervised learning, and reinforcement learning techniques. The subsection explores various machine learning algorithms, such as decision trees, support vector machines, neural networks, and deep learning. Readers also gain insights into the importance of data preparation and feature engineering in machine learning.

AI Applications across Industries:

The subsection explores the applications of AI across various industries and domains. Readers gain insights into how AI is transforming healthcare by enabling diagnosis, personalized treatment, and drug discovery. They explore the impact of AI in finance, where it facilitates fraud detection, algorithmic trading, and risk assessment. Readers also delve into AI applications in manufacturing, transportation, customer service, and marketing, among others. The subsection highlights the potential benefits of AI in improving efficiency, reducing costs, and enhancing decision-making processes in these industries.

Ethical Considerations in AI:

AI raises important ethical considerations, and the subsection emphasizes the significance of responsible AI development and deployment. Readers explore topics such as bias in AI algorithms, privacy concerns, transparency, and the impact of AI on jobs and society. They gain insights into the need for fair and accountable AI systems, explainability in AI decision-making, and human oversight in critical applications. The subsection emphasizes the importance of ethical frameworks and regulations to guide the development and use of AI technologies.

Future Directions in AI:

The subsection provides an overview of future directions in AI research and development. Readers explore emerging trends such as Explainable AI (XAI), AI in edge computing, federated learning, and AI-driven automation. They gain insights into the potential of AI in addressing complex societal challenges, fostering innovation, and shaping the future of work. The subsection highlights the need for ongoing research, collaboration, and responsible adoption of AI technologies to unlock their full potential.

Understanding Artificial Intelligence (AI) and Machine Learning is crucial for organizations to harness the transformative power of intelligent systems. Knowledge of AI concepts, machine learning techniques, applications across industries, ethical considerations, and future trends equips readers with the necessary tools to embrace and leverage AI effectively. It provides a foundation for exploring the potential of AI in addressing real-world challenges, optimizing processes, and driving innovation.

The section on Artificial Intelligence (AI) and Machine Learning emphasizes the significant impact of AI on various sectors and the potential it holds for innovation and transformation. It highlights the benefits of AI in improving decision-making, enhancing efficiency, and driving business growth. This understanding prepares readers to navigate the evolving landscape of AI and make informed decisions regarding AI adoption and integration into their organizations.

Internet of Things (IoT)

The Internet of Things (IoT) is a revolutionary concept that has transformed the way we interact with technology and the world around us. The section provides readers with a comprehensive understanding of IoT and its significant impact on various industries and domains.

Introduction to the Internet of Things (IoT):

The subsection begins by introducing readers to the concept of the Internet of Things. Readers gain insights into the purpose of IoT, which is to connect physical objects and devices to the internet, enabling them to collect and exchange data. They learn about the components of an IoT system, including sensors, actuators, connectivity technologies, and data processing platforms. The subsection explores the growth of IoT and its potential to transform industries, improve efficiency, and enhance the quality of life.

IoT Infrastructure and Technologies:

Readers delve into the essential infrastructure and technologies that enable IoT systems. They gain an understanding of the importance of wireless communication protocols, such as Wi-Fi, Bluetooth, and Zigbee, in facilitating seamless connectivity between devices. They explore cloud computing and edge computing technologies, which enable data storage, processing, and analysis in IoT systems. The subsection highlights the significance of data security, privacy, and encryption in IoT to protect sensitive information.

IoT Applications across Industries:

The subsection explores the diverse applications of IoT across various industries and domains. Readers gain insights into how IoT is transforming agriculture, healthcare, transportation, manufacturing, smart cities, and energy management, among others. They learn about precision agriculture techniques, remote patient monitoring in healthcare, smart transportation systems, predictive maintenance in manufacturing, and intelligent infrastructure in smart cities. The subsection highlights the potential benefits of IoT in optimizing processes, reducing costs, and improving sustainability.

Data Analytics and Insights:

IoT generates a massive amount of data, and readers explore the significance of data analytics in extracting valuable insights from IoT-generated data. They gain insights into the challenges of processing and analyzing big data in IoT systems and the role of data analytics techniques, such as machine learning and predictive modeling, in deriving actionable insights. The subsection emphasizes the importance of real-time analytics in IoT applications to enable timely decision-making.

Challenges and Considerations in IoT:

The subsection discusses the challenges and considerations associated with implementing and managing IoT systems. Readers explore topics such as data security, privacy concerns, interoperability, scalability, and device management. They gain insights into the importance of adopting robust security measures, ensuring data integrity, and complying with regulations and standards in IoT deployments. The subsection emphasizes the need for robust governance and risk management strategies to address these challenges effectively.

Future Directions in IoT:

The subsection provides an overview of emerging trends and future developments in the field of IoT. Readers explore topics such as 5G connectivity, edge computing, artificial intelligence integration, and IoT platforms. They gain insights into the potential of these advancements to enhance the capabilities and effectiveness of IoT systems. The subsection highlights the importance of interdisciplinary research, collaboration, and innovation to drive the evolution and adoption of IoT technologies.

Understanding the Internet of Things (IoT) is crucial for organizations to leverage the transformative potential of interconnected devices and systems. Knowledge of IoT concepts, infrastructure, applications across industries, data analytics, challenges, and future trends equips readers with the necessary tools to embrace and utilize IoT effectively. It provides a foundation for exploring the potential of IoT in optimizing processes, improving decision-making, and driving innovation.

The section on the Internet of Things (IoT) emphasizes the significant impact of IoT on various sectors and the potential it holds for improving efficiency and quality of life. It highlights the benefits of IoT in creating smart, connected ecosystems and driving sustainable development. This understanding prepares readers to embrace IoT technologies, address challenges, and make informed decisions regarding IoT integration and implementation within their organizations.

Blockchain Technology

Blockchain technology has gained significant attention and is considered a transformative force across various industries. This section provides readers with a comprehensive understanding of blockchain and its significant impact on various domains.

Introduction to Blockchain Technology:

The subsection begins by introducing readers to the concept of blockchain technology. Readers gain insights into the purpose of blockchain, which is to create a decentralized and immutable ledger that records transactions in a transparent and secure manner. They learn about the fundamental principles of blockchain, including distributed consensus, cryptographic techniques, and data immutability. The subsection explores the historical background of blockchain, its evolution from cryptocurrencies like Bitcoin, and its potential beyond finance.

Characteristics of Blockchain:

Readers delve into the key characteristics that define blockchain technology. They gain an understanding of decentralization, which eliminates the need for a central authority and allows for peer-to-peer transactions. They explore the concept of immutability, which ensures that once a transaction is recorded on the blockchain, it cannot be altered. Readers also explore transparency, as blockchain provides visibility of transactions to all participants. The subsection emphasizes the significance of these characteristics in building trust, security, and efficiency in various applications.

Blockchain Architecture and Components:

The subsection explores the architecture and components of a blockchain network. Readers gain insights into the structure of a blockchain, consisting of blocks that contain a set of transactions linked through cryptographic hashes. They learn about the role of consensus mechanisms, such as Proof of Work (PoW) and Proof of Stake (PoS), in validating and adding blocks to the blockchain. The subsection discusses the importance of cryptographic techniques, such as digital signatures and hash functions, in securing the integrity of transactions and ensuring data privacy.

Blockchain Applications:

Readers explore the diverse applications of blockchain technology across various domains. They gain insights into how blockchain is transforming industries such as supply chain management, healthcare, finance, real estate, voting systems, and intellectual property. They learn about the potential benefits of blockchain, including increased transparency, reduced fraud, enhanced traceability, and streamlined processes. The subsection highlights the importance of blockchain in enabling trust and efficiency in multi-party transactions and data exchange.

Challenges and Considerations in Blockchain Implementation:

The subsection discusses the challenges and considerations associated with implementing and adopting blockchain technology. Readers explore topics such as scalability, interoperability, regulatory compliance, and energy consumption. They gain insights into the trade-offs between decentralization and scalability and the need for industry standards and regulatory frameworks to foster blockchain adoption. The subsection emphasizes the importance of selecting appropriate consensus mechanisms and understanding the specific requirements of each use case.

Future Directions in Blockchain:

The subsection provides an overview of emerging trends and future developments in the field of blockchain. Readers explore topics such as scalability solutions, interoperability protocols, tokenization, and smart contracts. They gain insights into the potential of these advancements to enhance the capabilities and effectiveness of blockchain networks. The subsection highlights the importance of continued research, collaboration, and innovation to overcome existing challenges and unlock the full potential of blockchain technology.

Understanding Blockchain Technology is crucial for organizations to leverage its transformative potential and explore new possibilities in various domains. Knowledge of blockchain concepts, characteristics, architecture, applications, challenges, and future trends equips readers with the necessary tools to embrace and utilize blockchain effectively. It provides a foundation for exploring the potential of blockchain in improving transparency, security, and efficiency in various processes.

The section on Blockchain Technology emphasizes the significant impact of blockchain on various sectors and the potential it holds for revolutionizing traditional systems. It highlights the benefits of blockchain in enabling trust, reducing intermediaries, and creating new business models. This understanding prepares readers to embrace blockchain technologies, address challenges, and make informed decisions regarding blockchain integration and implementation within their organizations.

Virtual Reality (VR) and Augmented Reality (AR)

Virtual Reality (VR) and Augmented Reality (AR) are immersive technologies that have transformed the way we perceive and interact with the digital world. This section provides readers with a comprehensive understanding of VR and AR and their significant impact across various domains.

Introduction to Virtual Reality (VR) and Augmented Reality (AR):

The subsection begins by introducing readers to the concepts of Virtual Reality (VR) and Augmented Reality (AR). Readers gain insights into VR, which creates a simulated, immersive environment that can be explored and interacted with using specialized hardware, such as headsets and motion controllers. They also learn about AR, which overlays digital content onto the real world, enhancing the perception of reality through devices like smartphones or smart glasses. The subsection explores the evolution of VR and AR technologies and their potential to transform industries and experiences.

Virtual Reality (VR):

Readers delve into the realm of Virtual Reality (VR). They explore the hardware components of VR systems, including headsets, controllers, and tracking systems that enable users to immerse themselves in virtual environments. They gain insights into the various applications of VR across industries such as gaming, education, training simulations, architecture, healthcare, and entertainment. The subsection highlights the potential of VR in providing realistic and immersive experiences, enhancing learning and training, and fostering creativity.

Augmented Reality (AR):

The subsection explores the world of Augmented Reality (AR). Readers gain insights into AR technologies that overlay digital content onto the real world, enhancing the user's perception and interaction with their environment. They learn about marker-based AR, markerless AR, and location-based AR, along with the hardware and software components that enable AR experiences. Readers explore the applications of AR in fields such as education, healthcare, retail, manufacturing, and tourism. The subsection emphasizes the potential of AR in enhancing real-world experiences, providing interactive guidance and information, and improving productivity and efficiency.

Virtual Reality (VR) and Augmented Reality (AR) in Practice:

Readers gain insights into real-world examples of VR and AR applications. They explore how VR is used in flight simulators, architectural design, virtual tours, and therapy for anxiety and phobias. They also delve into AR applications such as overlaying digital information on real-world objects, interactive museum exhibits, and virtual try-on experiences in e-commerce. The subsection highlights the benefits of VR and AR in enhancing engagement, improving understanding, and providing immersive experiences.

Challenges and Considerations in VR and AR:

The subsection discusses the challenges and considerations associated with implementing and adopting VR and AR technologies. Readers explore topics such as hardware limitations, user comfort, content creation, ethical considerations, and privacy concerns. They gain insights into the importance of addressing these challenges to ensure widespread adoption and user acceptance of VR and AR experiences. The subsection emphasizes the need for user-centric design, accessibility, and responsible usage of VR and AR technologies.

Future Directions in VR and AR:

The subsection provides an overview of emerging trends and future developments in the field of VR and AR. Readers explore topics such as improved display technologies, haptic feedback, eye-tracking, and brain-computer interfaces. They gain insights into the potential of these advancements to enhance the realism, interactivity, and usability of VR and AR experiences. The subsection highlights the importance of ongoing research, technological advancements, and interdisciplinary collaboration to unlock the full potential of VR and AR technologies.

Understanding Virtual Reality (VR) and Augmented Reality (AR) is crucial for organizations to leverage their transformative potential and provide immersive experiences to users. Knowledge of VR and AR concepts, hardware components, applications, challenges, and future trends equips readers with the necessary tools to embrace and utilize VR and AR effectively. It provides a foundation for exploring the potential of VR and AR in various industries, from gaming and entertainment to education and healthcare.

The section on Virtual Reality (VR) and Augmented Reality (AR) emphasizes the significant impact of these immersive technologies on various sectors and the potential they hold for revolutionizing user experiences. It highlights the benefits of VR and AR in providing realistic simulations, enhancing understanding and engagement, and unlocking new opportunities for creativity and innovation. This understanding prepares readers to embrace VR and AR technologies, address challenges, and make informed decisions regarding their integration and implementation within their organizations.

CHAPTER 9: ICT AND SOCIETY

This chapter focuses on the social implications of Information and Communication Technology (ICT) and how it influences various aspects of society.

Digital Divide and Inclusion

This section explores the disparities in access to Information and Communication Technology (ICT) resources and the internet among different communities and regions. It sheds light on the concept of the digital divide and emphasizes the importance of digital inclusion to ensure equal opportunities for all individuals and communities.

Understanding the Digital Divide:

The subsection begins by explaining the concept of the digital divide. It refers to the gap between those who have access to ICT resources, such as computers, internet connectivity, and digital literacy, and those who do not. The digital divide is influenced by various factors, including socio-economic status, geographical location, education level, age, and gender. Readers gain insights into how these factors contribute to unequal access to technology and the internet, creating a divide in terms of digital skills, opportunities, and socio-economic development.

Dimensions of the Digital Divide:

Readers explore the different dimensions of the digital divide. It includes both the "access divide" and the "usage divide." The access divide refers to the disparity in physical access to ICT infrastructure, including reliable internet connectivity and computing devices. It encompasses factors such as infrastructure availability, affordability, and geographic coverage. The usage divide, on the other hand, focuses on the disparities in the utilization of ICT resources and digital literacy skills. It encompasses factors such as knowledge, skills, and attitudes towards technology.

Impact of the Digital Divide:

The subsection delves into the impact of the digital divide on individuals, communities, and societies as a whole. It highlights how the digital divide exacerbates existing inequalities, hindering socio-economic development, educational opportunities, and access to essential services. Individuals without access to technology face limitations in accessing information, educational resources, job opportunities, and government services. The digital divide can widen the gap between the privileged and marginalized populations, perpetuating social, economic, and educational inequalities.

Bridging the Digital Divide:

The subsection emphasizes the importance of bridging the digital divide through digital inclusion initiatives. It explores various strategies and approaches to promote equal access to technology and the internet. Governments, non-profit organizations, and private sector entities play a crucial role in implementing policies and programs to provide affordable internet access, improve digital literacy, and enhance ICT infrastructure in underserved areas. Readers also gain insights into the significance of public-private partnerships, community engagement, and educational initiatives to bridge the digital divide effectively.

Benefits of Digital Inclusion:

The subsection highlights the numerous benefits of digital inclusion. When individuals and communities have access to ICT resources and digital literacy skills, they can leverage technology for personal growth, educational advancement, economic opportunities, and civic engagement. Digital inclusion empowers individuals to access online education, remote work opportunities, e-government services, and healthcare information. It fosters innovation, creativity, and economic development in underserved areas. Moreover, digital inclusion contributes to social cohesion, democratic participation, and bridging societal gaps.

Ensuring Sustainable Digital Inclusion:

The subsection emphasizes the importance of ensuring sustainable digital inclusion. It explores the need for long-term strategies, policies, and investments to bridge the digital divide effectively. It highlights the significance of equitable distribution of resources, affordable connectivity options, digital skills training, and community engagement. Readers gain insights into the importance of addressing the socio-economic barriers that contribute to the digital divide, such as poverty, gender inequality, and limited access to education.

Understanding the concept of the digital divide and the importance of digital inclusion is crucial for individuals, policymakers, and organizations to address inequalities and promote equitable access to technology. Knowledge of the dimensions of the digital divide, its impact, strategies for bridging the divide, and the benefits of digital inclusion equips readers with the necessary tools to advocate for and contribute to digital inclusion initiatives.

The section on Digital Divide and Inclusion emphasizes the significance of bridging the digital divide to ensure equal opportunities and access to ICT resources for all individuals and communities. It highlights the potential of technology to empower individuals, foster economic development, and promote social cohesion. This understanding prepares readers to address the challenges of the digital divide, promote digital inclusion, and contribute to a more inclusive and equitable digital society.

Ethical and Legal Considerations in ICT

This section explores the ethical and legal implications of Information and Communication Technology (ICT) use. It highlights the importance of ethical frameworks, principles, and legal regulations to guide responsible ICT practices and foster trust in the digital realm.

Ethical Frameworks in ICT:

The subsection begins by introducing readers to ethical frameworks in ICT. It explores the principles that guide ethical behavior in technology-related contexts, such as privacy, transparency, accountability, fairness, and responsibility. Readers gain insights into the importance of considering ethical implications in the design, development, and deployment of ICT systems. They learn about the ethical challenges that arise with emerging technologies, such as artificial intelligence, data analytics, and automation. The subsection emphasizes the significance of applying ethical frameworks to promote responsible and sustainable ICT practices.

Intellectual Property Rights:

Readers delve into the ethical and legal considerations related to intellectual property in the ICT domain. They gain insights into copyright laws, patents, trademarks, and trade secrets that protect creative works, inventions, and innovations. The subsection highlights the importance of respecting intellectual property rights and ensuring proper attribution and licensing of digital content. It explores the challenges of intellectual property infringement in the digital age and the ethical implications of unauthorized copying, distribution, and use of intellectual property.

Digital Rights and Access to Information:

The subsection explores the ethical considerations related to digital rights and access to information. Readers gain insights into the importance of freedom of expression, privacy rights, and access to information in the digital realm. They explore topics such as net neutrality, censorship, surveillance, and government transparency. The subsection emphasizes the significance of safeguarding individuals' digital rights, ensuring freedom of speech, and promoting open access to information while respecting privacy and security.

Ethical Use of Data:

Readers delve into the ethical considerations related to data collection, storage, and usage in ICT systems. They gain insights into the ethical implications of data practices, such as data privacy, informed consent, data anonymization, and the responsible use of personal and sensitive data. The subsection explores the challenges of data breaches, data monetization, and algorithmic biases. It emphasizes the importance of transparency, data governance, and user empowerment in ethical data management practices.

Responsible AI and Automation:

The subsection highlights the ethical considerations associated with artificial intelligence (AI) and automation. Readers gain insights into the ethical challenges of AI decision-making, algorithmic biases, and the potential impact on employment and society. They explore topics such as AI transparency, accountability, explainability, and the ethical use of AI in critical domains such as healthcare and finance. The subsection emphasizes the significance of ensuring responsible AI development, addressing biases, and preserving human values and rights in the design and deployment of AI systems.

Legal Regulations and Compliance:

The subsection discusses the legal regulations and compliance requirements in the ICT domain. Readers explore topics such as data protection laws, privacy regulations, cybersecurity standards, and consumer protection laws. They gain insights into the importance of complying with legal frameworks to protect individuals' rights, ensure data privacy and security, and prevent fraudulent practices. The subsection emphasizes the need for organizations to understand and adhere to applicable laws and regulations to foster trust and avoid legal repercussions.

Understanding the ethical and legal considerations in ICT is crucial for individuals, organizations, and policymakers to navigate the complex landscape of technology responsibly. Knowledge of ethical frameworks, intellectual property rights, digital rights, responsible data practices, and legal compliance equips readers with the necessary tools to make informed decisions and promote ethical and lawful ICT practices.

The section on Ethical and Legal Considerations in ICT emphasizes the significance of ethical conduct and legal compliance in the adoption and use of ICT. It highlights the importance of respecting intellectual property, preserving digital rights, ensuring privacy and data protection, and fostering responsible AI and automation. This understanding prepares readers to navigate ethical and legal challenges, advocate for ethical practices, and contribute to a trustworthy and sustainable digital environment.

Privacy and Data Protection

This section explores the importance of safeguarding privacy and protecting personal data in the digital age. It sheds light on the ethical and legal considerations related to privacy and data protection, highlighting the need to balance the benefits of technology with individuals' rights to privacy and control over their personal information.

Understanding Privacy:

The subsection begins by explaining the concept of privacy in the digital context. It explores the importance of privacy as a fundamental human right and its significance in maintaining autonomy, dignity, and personal security. Readers gain insights into the challenges posed by technological advancements, such as data collection, surveillance, and profiling, to individuals' privacy. They explore the different dimensions of privacy, including informational privacy, bodily privacy, and privacy in public spaces.

Personal Data and its Protection:

Readers delve into the concept of personal data and its protection. They gain insights into the types of personal data collected in the digital realm, including demographic information, online activities, biometric data, and geolocation data. The subsection explores the ethical considerations related to data collection, storage, and usage, emphasizing the need for informed consent, purpose limitation, data minimization, and data accuracy. Readers also explore the legal frameworks and regulations, such as the General Data Protection Regulation (GDPR), that aim to protect individuals' rights and ensure responsible data practices.

Data Privacy Challenges:

The subsection highlights the challenges associated with data privacy in the digital age. Readers explore topics such as data breaches, unauthorized access, data sharing practices, and the potential misuse of personal data. They gain insights into the risks of identity theft, financial fraud, and the potential impact on individuals' reputation and well-being. The subsection emphasizes the importance of adopting security measures, such as encryption, access controls, and data anonymization, to protect personal data from unauthorized access and mitigate privacy risks.

Privacy by Design and Default:

Readers delve into the concept of privacy by design and default, which emphasizes the integration of privacy considerations into the design and development of ICT systems. They gain insights into the principles of privacy by design, including data protection, user control, transparency, and accountability. The subsection highlights the significance of privacy-enhancing technologies, such as privacy-preserving algorithms, differential privacy, and secure data storage, in minimizing privacy risks and empowering individuals to maintain control over their personal information.

Individual Rights and Responsibilities:

The subsection emphasizes the rights and responsibilities of individuals in protecting their privacy and personal data. Readers gain insights into their rights to access, correct, and delete their personal information held by organizations. They explore the importance of being aware of privacy settings, managing consent preferences, and adopting safe online practices. The subsection emphasizes the role of digital literacy and education in empowering individuals to make informed decisions and protect their privacy rights.

Organizational Responsibilities:

The subsection discusses the responsibilities of organizations in ensuring privacy and data protection. Readers explore topics such as privacy policies, data protection impact assessments, and data breach notification requirements. They gain insights into the importance of implementing privacy and security measures, conducting regular audits, and complying with legal and regulatory requirements. The subsection emphasizes the significance of fostering a privacy-aware culture within organizations and promoting transparency and accountability in data practices.

Understanding privacy and data protection is crucial for individuals, organizations, and policymakers to navigate the digital landscape responsibly. Knowledge of privacy concepts, personal data protection, data privacy challenges, privacy by design, individual rights, and organizational responsibilities equips readers with the necessary tools to advocate for privacy rights and promote responsible data practices.

The section on Privacy and Data Protection emphasizes the significance of safeguarding individuals' privacy and protecting personal data in the digital age. It highlights the importance of privacy as a fundamental human right and the need for ethical and legal frameworks to guide data practices. This understanding prepares readers to address privacy challenges, advocate for privacy-enhancing technologies, and contribute to a privacy-respecting and data-secure digital environment.

Cybersecurity and Online Threats

The section explores the importance of cybersecurity in the digital landscape and addresses the various online threats that individuals, organizations, and societies face. It sheds light on the ethical and legal considerations associated with cybersecurity and emphasizes the need for proactive measures to protect against online threats.

Understanding Cybersecurity:

The subsection begins by explaining the concept of cybersecurity and its significance in the digital age. Readers gain insights into the importance of protecting information systems, networks, and digital assets from unauthorized access, disruption, and damage. They explore the principles of cybersecurity, including prevention, detection, response, and recovery. The subsection emphasizes the need for robust cybersecurity measures to safeguard sensitive information, maintain trust, and ensure the continuity of operations.

Online Threats:

Readers delve into the various online threats that individuals and organizations encounter. They gain insights into common cyber threats such as malware, ransomware, phishing attacks, social engineering, and distributed denial-of-service (DDoS) attacks. The subsection explores the techniques used by cybercriminals to exploit vulnerabilities in systems and networks, compromise data, and gain unauthorized access. Readers also explore the emerging threats in the digital landscape, such as insider threats, IoT vulnerabilities, and advanced persistent threats (APTs).

Security Measures:

The subsection discusses the security measures that individuals and organizations can adopt to mitigate cyber risks. Readers explore topics such as network security, endpoint protection, encryption, access controls, and vulnerability management. They gain insights into the importance of implementing robust security protocols, keeping software up to date, and conducting regular security assessments. The subsection emphasizes the significance of user awareness training and secure coding practices to prevent common attack vectors and minimize security breaches.

Data Breaches and Incident Response:

Readers delve into the topic of data breaches and incident response. They gain insights into the ethical and legal considerations associated with data breaches, including the potential impact on individuals' privacy and the legal obligations for reporting and notifying affected parties. The subsection highlights the importance of incident response plans, which outline the steps to be taken in the event of a cybersecurity incident. Readers explore the significance of timely detection, containment, investigation, and recovery to minimize the impact of data breaches.

Ethical Hacking and Penetration Testing:

The subsection explores the concept of ethical hacking and penetration testing as proactive measures to identify vulnerabilities in systems and networks. Readers gain insights into the role of ethical hackers, also known as white-hat hackers, in identifying weaknesses and reporting them to organizations to enhance security. They explore the ethical and legal considerations associated with penetration testing and the importance of conducting regular security assessments to identify and address vulnerabilities before they are exploited by malicious actors.

Collaborative Approaches to Cybersecurity:

The subsection emphasizes the importance of collaboration and information sharing in combating cyber threats. Readers explore the role of public-private partnerships, industry collaboration, and government initiatives in promoting cybersecurity best practices, threat intelligence sharing, and incident response coordination. The subsection highlights the significance of global cooperation to address cybercrime, develop international standards, and foster a secure digital ecosystem.

Understanding cybersecurity and online threats is crucial for individuals, organizations, and policymakers to navigate the digital landscape securely. Knowledge of cybersecurity principles, common online threats, security measures, incident response, ethical hacking, and collaboration equips readers with the necessary tools to proactively protect against cyber risks and respond effectively to cybersecurity incidents.

The section on Cybersecurity and Online Threats emphasizes the significance of adopting robust cybersecurity measures, promoting user awareness, and fostering collaborative efforts to combat cyber threats. It highlights the importance of ethical and legal considerations in cybersecurity practices and the need for a comprehensive and proactive approach to safeguarding digital assets and maintaining trust in the digital realm. This understanding prepares readers to address cybersecurity challenges, promote secure practices, and contribute to a resilient and secure digital environment.

CHAPTER 10: FUTURE TRENDS AND INNOVATIONS

This chapter explores the future trends and innovations in the field of Information and Communication Technology (ICT). It sheds light on the emerging technologies and their potential impact on various sectors, including smart cities, quantum computing, next-generation networks, and the role of ICT in healthcare, education, and governance.

Smart Cities and Sustainable ICT

This section explores the concept of smart cities and the role of sustainable ICT in transforming urban environments. It sheds light on the integration of various technologies and data-driven solutions to enhance the quality of life, sustainability, and efficiency of cities.

Understanding Smart Cities:

The subsection begins by introducing readers to the concept of smart cities. It explains that smart cities leverage Information and Communication Technology (ICT) to collect and analyze data from various sources, including sensors, devices, and infrastructure, to improve the functioning of urban environments. Readers gain insights into the interconnected nature of smart city systems, which encompass domains such as transportation, energy, water management, waste management, public safety, and governance. The subsection highlights the goals of smart cities, which include enhancing citizen well-being, optimizing resource utilization, improving infrastructure, and promoting sustainability.

Technologies and Components of Smart Cities:

Readers delve into the technologies and components that contribute to the functioning of smart cities. They explore the Internet of Things (IoT), which enables the connection and communication of devices and sensors to collect and exchange data. They gain insights into the role of data analytics and artificial intelligence in processing and deriving meaningful insights from the collected data. The subsection also highlights the significance of connectivity infrastructure, such as high-speed networks and wireless communication, to facilitate seamless data exchange. Readers explore the role of smart grids, smart buildings, intelligent transportation systems, and smart sensors in creating a connected and sustainable urban ecosystem.

Benefits of Smart Cities:

The subsection explores the benefits that smart cities offer to residents, businesses, and governments. Readers gain insights into the potential advantages of smart cities, such as improved energy efficiency, optimized transportation systems, reduced traffic congestion, enhanced public safety, efficient waste management, and enhanced citizen participation. They also explore the potential economic benefits, including job creation, innovation, and increased competitiveness. The subsection emphasizes the potential of smart cities to improve the quality of life, promote sustainable development, and address urban challenges effectively.

Sustainable ICT Practices:

The subsection highlights the importance of sustainable ICT practices in the development and operation of smart cities. Readers explore topics such as energy-efficient ICT infrastructure, renewable energy integration, and green data centers. They gain insights into the significance of responsible e-waste management, recycling, and lifecycle assessment of ICT equipment. The subsection emphasizes the need for energy-efficient buildings, smart grid integration, and sustainable transportation systems to minimize the environmental impact of smart city initiatives. It also explores the potential of citizen engagement, education, and behavior change to foster sustainable practices in smart cities.

Challenges and Considerations:

The subsection discusses the challenges and considerations associated with the implementation of smart city initiatives. Readers explore topics such as data privacy and security, ensuring interoperability and data sharing among different systems, addressing digital divides and inclusivity, and balancing the benefits of technology with social and ethical considerations. The subsection emphasizes the need for comprehensive planning, stakeholder collaboration, and citizen participation to address these challenges effectively.

Understanding the concept of smart cities and the role of sustainable ICT is crucial for urban planners, policymakers, and technology providers to shape the cities of the future. Knowledge of smart city technologies, benefits, sustainable ICT practices, and the challenges involved equips readers with the necessary tools to develop and implement smart city strategies that are socially inclusive, environmentally sustainable, and technologically efficient.

The section on Smart Cities and Sustainable ICT emphasizes the potential of ICT solutions to transform urban environments and improve the quality of life for citizens. It highlights the importance of sustainable practices to minimize the environmental impact of technology deployment. This understanding prepares readers to explore innovative approaches, address challenges, and contribute to the development of smart cities that are resilient, inclusive, and sustainable.

Quantum Computing

This section explores the emerging field of quantum computing and its potential to revolutionize computation. It delves into the fundamental principles of quantum mechanics and how they can be harnessed to perform complex computational tasks.

Introduction to Quantum Computing:

The subsection begins by introducing readers to the concept of quantum computing. It explains that quantum computing utilizes the principles of quantum mechanics to perform computations using quantum bits, or qubits. Readers gain insights into the fundamental differences between classical computing and quantum computing, including the concepts of superposition and entanglement. They explore the potential of quantum computing to solve problems that are currently intractable for classical computers, such as cryptography, optimization, and simulation of quantum systems.

Quantum Mechanics Principles:

Readers delve into the principles of quantum mechanics that underpin quantum computing. They gain insights into concepts such as superposition, which allows qubits to exist in multiple states simultaneously, and entanglement, which describes the correlation between qubits that enables instantaneous information transfer. The subsection explores the significance of quantum gates, which manipulate qubits to perform quantum computations. Readers also explore the concept of quantum parallelism, which enables quantum computers to perform computations on multiple inputs simultaneously, providing exponential computational power for certain tasks.

Challenges in Quantum Computing:

The subsection discusses the challenges associated with quantum computing. Readers gain insights into the inherent fragility of qubits, which are sensitive to environmental noise and decoherence. They explore the efforts to develop error correction codes and fault-tolerant systems to address these challenges. The subsection also highlights the current limitations of quantum computers in terms of the number of qubits, gate error rates, and scalability. Readers gain an understanding of the ongoing research and development in the field to overcome these challenges and realize the full potential of quantum computing.

Potential Applications of Quantum Computing:

The subsection explores the potential applications of quantum computing across various domains. Readers gain insights into the potential impact of quantum computing on fields such as cryptography, optimization, material science, drug discovery, and financial modeling. They explore how quantum algorithms can provide significant speedup and efficiency for solving complex problems, which are otherwise computationally expensive or infeasible for classical computers. The subsection also highlights the collaborative efforts between researchers, industry leaders, and governments to explore and harness the potential of quantum computing.

Ethical and Societal Considerations:

The subsection discusses the ethical and societal considerations associated with quantum computing. Readers explore topics such as quantum cryptography and the potential impact on encryption methods, quantum supremacy and its implications for traditional computing, and the need for responsible development and use of quantum technologies. The subsection emphasizes the importance of considering the ethical implications of quantum computing, ensuring the security and privacy of quantum systems, and addressing the potential societal impacts of quantum advancements.

Understanding the principles and potential of quantum computing is crucial for researchers, technologists, and policymakers to navigate the future of computing. Knowledge of quantum mechanics principles, challenges, potential applications, and ethical considerations equips readers with the necessary tools to contribute to the advancement of quantum computing and explore its transformative potential.

The section on Quantum Computing emphasizes the significance of quantum technologies in revolutionizing computation and addressing complex problems. It highlights the ongoing research and development in the field and the collaborative efforts to explore quantum algorithms and applications. This understanding prepares readers to embrace the potential of quantum computing, anticipate its impact across various domains, and contribute to the ethical and responsible development of quantum technologies.

5G and Beyond

This section explores the next generation of wireless communication networks and their potential to transform connectivity and enable new applications. It delves into the features, capabilities, and potential impact of 5G networks, as well as the future developments beyond 5G.

Introduction to 5G:

The subsection begins by introducing readers to the concept of 5G, the fifth generation of wireless communication technology. It explains that 5G networks offer significant improvements over their predecessors, including higher data transfer rates, lower latency, greater capacity, and increased device connectivity. Readers gain insights into the key technologies that enable 5G, such as millimeter-wave frequencies, massive multiple-input multiple-output (MIMO), and network slicing. The subsection highlights the potential of 5G to support a wide range of applications, from autonomous vehicles and smart cities to augmented reality and remote surgery.

Key Features and Capabilities of 5G:

Readers delve into the key features and capabilities of 5G networks. They gain insights into the ultra-fast data transfer rates, which can reach up to multi-gigabit speeds, enabling real-time communication and high-quality multimedia streaming. They explore the significantly reduced latency of 5G, which enables near-instantaneous response times, critical for applications like autonomous vehicles and virtual reality. The subsection also discusses the increased device connectivity and capacity of 5G networks, allowing for the seamless integration of billions of connected devices in the Internet of Things (IoT) ecosystem.

Applications and Potential Impact of 5G:

The subsection explores the potential impact of 5G across various sectors and applications. Readers gain insights into how 5G networks can revolutionize industries such as healthcare, transportation, manufacturing, and entertainment. They explore how 5G can enable telemedicine, remote patient monitoring, smart transportation systems, industrial automation, and immersive experiences through augmented and virtual reality. The subsection highlights the potential economic benefits of 5G, including job creation, innovation, and increased productivity. It emphasizes the transformative potential of 5G in enabling new business models and driving digital transformation.

Beyond 5G Developments:

The subsection discusses the future developments beyond 5G. Readers gain insights into the ongoing research and development efforts to enhance wireless communication technology further. They explore concepts such as terahertz communication, which utilizes higher frequency bands for even faster data transfer rates. They also delve into the potential of satellite-based networks to provide global connectivity, particularly in underserved areas. The subsection highlights the importance of continued innovation and collaboration to realize the full potential of wireless communication technology beyond 5G.

Infrastructure, Standards, and Challenges:

The subsection discusses the infrastructure, standards, and challenges associated with 5G and beyond. Readers explore topics such as the deployment of 5G infrastructure, spectrum allocation, and the need for robust and reliable network coverage. They gain insights into the international standards and interoperability considerations to ensure seamless connectivity across different networks and regions. The subsection also addresses the challenges of security, privacy, and potential health concerns related to the deployment of 5G networks.

Understanding the advancements in wireless communication technology, particularly 5G and beyond, is crucial for individuals, organizations, and policymakers to leverage the potential of connectivity and enable new applications. Knowledge of the features and capabilities of 5G, its potential impact across various sectors, and the ongoing developments beyond 5G equips readers with the necessary tools to navigate the evolving landscape of wireless communication technology.

The section on 5G and Beyond emphasizes the significance of 5G networks in transforming connectivity and enabling innovative applications. It highlights the potential economic, societal, and technological benefits of 5G, as well as the future developments beyond 5G. This understanding prepares readers to embrace the opportunities of 5G, contribute to the development of wireless communication technology, and explore its transformative potential across industries and sectors.

The Role of ICT in Healthcare, Education, and Governance

This section explores the transformative potential of Information and Communication Technology (ICT) in these crucial sectors. It sheds light on how ICT advancements can revolutionize healthcare delivery, education systems, and governance practices.

ICT in Healthcare:

The subsection begins by discussing the role of ICT in healthcare. It explores how ICT solutions, such as electronic health records, telemedicine, and remote patient monitoring, can enhance healthcare delivery and improve patient outcomes. Readers gain insights into the potential benefits of ICT in healthcare, including improved access to healthcare services, enhanced communication between healthcare professionals and patients, and better coordination of care. The subsection highlights the potential of wearable devices, health apps, and artificial intelligence in empowering individuals to take control of their health and enabling personalized medicine.

ICT in Education:

Readers delve into the role of ICT in education. They explore how ICT solutions, such as e-learning platforms, virtual classrooms, and educational apps, can transform traditional education systems. The subsection discusses the potential of ICT to increase access to quality education, particularly in remote or underserved areas. Readers gain insights into how ICT can facilitate personalized learning experiences, foster collaboration and engagement, and provide diverse educational resources. The subsection also explores the role of ICT in lifelong learning, professional development, and upskilling in the digital age.

ICT in Governance:

The subsection highlights the role of ICT in governance practices. Readers gain insights into how ICT solutions can improve government services, streamline administrative processes, and enhance citizen engagement. They explore the potential of e-government services, such as online portals, digital signatures, and electronic voting systems, to improve the efficiency and transparency of government operations. The subsection also discusses the potential of ICT in data-driven decision making, open data initiatives, and digital democracy, enabling greater citizen participation and accountability.

Challenges and Considerations:

The subsection addresses the challenges and considerations associated with the role of ICT in healthcare, education, and governance. Readers explore topics such as data privacy and security, digital divides, accessibility, and the need for digital literacy. They gain insights into the ethical and legal considerations in handling sensitive health information, protecting student data, and ensuring the inclusivity of ICT solutions. The subsection emphasizes the importance of addressing these challenges through appropriate policies, regulations, and capacity-building initiatives.

Understanding the role of ICT in healthcare, education, and governance is crucial for individuals, policymakers, and organizations to leverage the potential of technology for positive societal impact. Knowledge of ICT solutions, their benefits, challenges, and considerations equips readers with the necessary tools to contribute to the advancement and responsible use of ICT in these sectors.

The section on the Role of ICT in Healthcare, Education, and Governance emphasizes the transformative potential of ICT solutions in revolutionizing these crucial sectors. It highlights the importance of leveraging ICT for improved healthcare delivery, accessible education, and effective governance practices. This understanding prepares readers to embrace ICT advancements, advocate for inclusive and responsible ICT practices, and contribute to creating a digitally empowered society.

CONCLUSION: EMBRACING THE ICT REVOLUTION

The conclusion brings together the key concepts, technologies, challenges, and opportunities discussed throughout the book. It emphasizes the importance of harnessing the power of ICT to shape a better future for individuals, organizations, and societies.

Recap of Key Concepts and Technologies:

The conclusion begins with a recap of the key concepts and technologies explored in the book. It revisits the fundamental principles of ICT, including hardware, software, networking, programming, databases, and emerging technologies. Readers are reminded of the significance of understanding these concepts and how they contribute to the advancement of ICT.

Challenges and Opportunities in the ICT Landscape:

The conclusion addresses the challenges and opportunities present in the ICT landscape. It acknowledges the rapid pace of technological advancements, which bring both benefits and complexities. Readers are reminded of the importance of addressing challenges such as cybersecurity, privacy, digital divide, ethical considerations, and the need for lifelong learning. The conclusion emphasizes the opportunities that arise from embracing ICT, including increased efficiency, innovation, economic growth, and improved quality of life.

Harnessing the Power of ICT for a Better Future:

The conclusion emphasizes the need to harness the power of ICT to create a better future. It highlights the transformative potential of ICT in various sectors, including healthcare, education, governance, business, and everyday life. Readers are encouraged to leverage ICT to address societal challenges, promote sustainability, foster inclusivity, and drive positive change. The conclusion emphasizes the role of individuals, organizations, and policymakers in responsibly using and shaping ICT for the benefit of all.

Continuous Learning and Adaptation:

The conclusion emphasizes the importance of continuous learning and adaptation in the ICT landscape. Readers are encouraged to stay informed about emerging technologies, industry trends, and best practices. They are reminded of the need to embrace lifelong learning, acquire digital literacy skills, and stay updated with ethical and legal considerations. The conclusion emphasizes that embracing the ICT revolution requires a mindset of adaptability and openness to change.

In conclusion, "Unleashing the Power of Information and Communication Technology: A Comprehensive Guide" provides readers with a comprehensive understanding of ICT and its various applications. The book explores the key concepts, technologies, challenges, and opportunities in the ICT landscape. It highlights the transformative potential of ICT and encourages readers to embrace the power of technology to shape a better future.

By harnessing the power of ICT, individuals, organizations, and societies can drive innovation, enhance productivity, improve service delivery, and foster positive social change. The conclusion reiterates the importance of responsible and inclusive use of ICT, as well as the need for continuous learning and adaptation. It leaves readers inspired to embrace the ICT revolution, contribute to its advancement, and create a world where technology empowers and benefits all.

GLOSSARY OF ICT TERMINOLOGY

This glossary provides a comprehensive list of commonly used Information and Communication Technology (ICT) terminology, helping readers understand and navigate the diverse vocabulary associated with ICT.

Artificial Intelligence (AI): The simulation of human intelligence in machines that can learn, reason, and perform tasks autonomously.

Big Data: Extremely large and complex data sets that require advanced techniques and technologies for processing, analysis, and visualization.

Cloud Computing: The delivery of computing resources, such as storage, servers, and software, over the internet, allowing users to access and use them on-demand.

Cybersecurity: The practice of protecting computer systems, networks, and data from unauthorized access, attacks, and other potential threats.

Data Mining: The process of discovering patterns, correlations, and insights from large datasets using various statistical and analytical techniques.

Encryption: The process of converting data into a form that is unreadable to unauthorized users, ensuring secure transmission and storage of sensitive information.

Internet of Things (IoT): A network of physical objects embedded with sensors, software, and connectivity, enabling them to collect and exchange data over the internet.

Machine Learning: A subset of AI that focuses on enabling machines to learn and improve from data and experiences without being explicitly programmed.

Network: A collection of interconnected devices, such as computers, servers, routers, and switches, that allows for the exchange of data and resources.

Programming: The process of creating computer programs using programming languages to provide instructions for computers to execute specific tasks.

Robotics: The interdisciplinary field that involves the design, development, and operation of robots and autonomous systems capable of performing tasks autonomously or with minimal human intervention.

Software: A collection of programs, data, and instructions that enable computers and other devices to perform specific tasks or functions.

User Interface (UI): The visual and interactive components of a software application or system that allow users to interact with and control the functionality.

Virtual Reality (VR): An immersive experience that simulates a realistic or imaginary environment using computer-generated sensory input, typically involving headsets and motion tracking.

Web Development: The process of creating and maintaining websites or web applications, involving the use of programming languages, markup languages, and web technologies.

Wi-Fi: A wireless communication technology that allows devices to connect to a local area network (LAN) or the internet wirelessly.

XML (eXtensible Markup Language): A markup language used for encoding and structuring data in a format that is both human-readable and machine-readable.

5G: The fifth generation of wireless communication technology that offers faster data transfer speeds, lower latency, and greater capacity compared to previous generations.

API (Application Programming Interface): A set of rules and protocols that enable different software applications to communicate and interact with each other.

Blockchain: A decentralized and distributed digital ledger technology that securely records and verifies transactions across multiple computers.

This glossary provides a starting point for understanding the diverse range of terms used in the field of ICT. It is important to note that ICT terminology is constantly evolving, and new terms and concepts continue to emerge as technology advances. Continuous learning and staying updated with the latest developments are key to staying knowledgeable in the dynamic world of ICT.

www.ingramcontent.com/pod-product-compliance
Lightning Source LLC
LaVergne TN
LVHW051344050326
832903LV00031B/3739